YANKEE BATBOY

The Luckiest Kid in New York

By

Anthony Florio and John Siclare

Printed in the United States of America at McNally Jackson Books, 52 Prince Street, New York, NY 10012.

First Edition

For Rosie the Bride

My Mom
Rose "Rosie" Florio

It's 1961 and I'm a fifteen year old kid living in Little Italy who eats, sleeps and drinks baseball; a kid who believes he's the biggest baseball fan that ever lived and idolizes Mickey Mantle. Try to imagine how it felt for a kid like this to be asked if he'd like to be a batboy at Yankee Stadium; to actually be around the famous ballplayers of the day. This is my story, and the excitement of walking into Yankee Stadium for the first time in my life, in the very same underground tunnels that Babe Ruth had walked through. It still excites me today whenever I think about it.

Foreword

In 1961 Anthony Florio, an inner-city kid from a working-class family in New York City, was given the opportunity of a lifetime; a chance to work at Yankee Stadium as a ball-boy for visiting teams. With the tumultuous 1960s as a backdrop, Anthony's story of how he later became batboy for the Yankees – working at the stadium, interacting with famous players and travelling with one of the greatest teams in sports history – is a warm and poignant memoir of one young man's very special life.

The global events, political turmoil, social changes and Cultural Revolution taking place in the early 1960s provided a fertile environment in which to grow up. The race for space was on, the winds of war were swirling in Southeast Asia, The Cuban Missile Crisis brought the world perilously close to a nuclear holocaust, the assassinations of President Kennedy, Martin Luther King and Robert Kennedy shocked the nation and the fight for civil rights and racial equality grew angrier and more violent. Culturally, the 1960s would bear witness to a transition in the performing arts. Frank Sinatra's voice was, arguably, at its purest and finest level, but he was part of an older generation. Elvis was still the King of rock and roll, the Beach Boys, Four Tops and Four Seasons topped the charts but the Beatles would soon change all of that. And following the Beatles would be the flower children, the drug culture and the sexual revolution.

Yet, as global, political and social events captured the world's attention and as cultural events consumed the attention of anyone over seventeen years of age, attention was, at the same time, also being paid to something else. In the hearts and minds of adolescent boys around the country, the very reason for living, the only thing other than your mother or father worth dying for was baseball.

The big cities had professional teams and some had more than one. Chicago had the White Sox and the Cubs, Boston had the Red Sox, Detroit had the Tigers, Baltimore had the Orioles, Los Angeles had the Dodgers, San Francisco had the Giants, Cleveland had the Indians; all great teams. If you were lucky enough to live in New York City in the 1960s, you had the greatest team on Earth; the New York Yankees. And if you were very lucky you'd have a chance to watch the Yankees play in one of the greatest ballparks in America, Yankee Stadium · the home of Babe Ruth, Lou Gehrig and Joe DiMaggio, and of course, Mickey Mantle.

In the 1960s, every kid in New York City who ever stepped up to home plate – drawn in chalk on the street or on a schoolyard wall – to play stickball, imagined himself as Mickey Mantle or Roger Maris or Yogi Berra or Elston Howard; every pitcher was Whitey Ford or Jim Bouton; every infielder was Clete Boyer or Bobby Richardson or Tony Kubek. The street became Yankee Stadium and the fire escapes and open windows became the stands; often filled with cheering relatives and neighbors. One self-imagined Mickey Mantle who was by his own admission, "a skinny 120lb weasel," loved the sport, idolized the professional ballplayers and dreamed incessantly about going to Yankee Stadium. This is the story of Anthony Florio, who in 1962 at the age of fifteen became the luckiest kid in New York.

Anthony Florio was the only child of Rose and Sal Florio. Sal was a truck driver; Rose was housewife and a loving mother to Anthony. The Florio family lived in a tenement building on Broome Street in the Little Italy neighborhood of the Borough of Manhattan. Little Italy was an absolutely unique environment for a young boy in the 1960s. Every mother knew every other mother's kid, and every kid was respectful to his or her parents. In the 1960s Little Italy was the safest neighborhood in New York City.

Anthony was a street-smart kid who found comfort in the City's Public School System. His grammar school, PS 130, provided a good education and an excellent social environment. One environment that had a lasting effect on Anthony would be found in another New York City Borough; the Bronx. In his spare time and on weekends, Sal Florio coached a sandlot baseball team in the Bronx called the New York Redwings. Anthony played for the Redwing Juniors and was a capable pitcher, once forcing future Hall of Famer Rod Carew to ground out to the second baseman. He became a good friend to his teammates, several of who went on to play professional baseball. Not only was Sal Florio an excellent coach, but by recruiting so many good ballplayers from around the city, major league scouts were attracted to the team and contracts were offered to such players as Ken Singleton, Ed Kranepool and Duke Carmel, as well as to dozens of other players.

As Anthony approached high school age Sal Florio had apprehensions about sending him to a public high school in Manhattan. Through his coaching activities Sal met the athletic director of James Monroe High School, Steve Ray. In addition to his role at James Monroe, Steve Ray was also a scout for the Chicago White Sox. Sal wanted Anthony to attend this Bronx high school while still living in Manhattan but Steve Ray could not help unless Anthony moved to the Bronx, so by substituting the Bronx residence of a friend and adopting it as his own, Anthony was able to attend James Monroe. Rather than maintaining a low profile in the Bronx, young Anthony tried out for the varsity baseball team and as a freshman, qualified and made the team. It was in his freshman year at James Monroe High School when Anthony's good fortune and incredible journey would begin. One afternoon between classes Anthony found his way to the gym to spend time with

Steve Ray. Anthony did not know that Steve Ray also had a relationship with the folks at Yankee Stadium. "Anthony, I've been asked to send some kids to Yankee Stadium" said Steve Ray "to try out for the position of ball boy during the games. Would you be interested in trying out?"

Anthony's reaction to this question, his life among the superstars of the day and the incredible events that filled his life from that moment in 1961 through the end of the 1964 Yankee season, are the experiences of a lifetime and are, 50 years later, the basis for Yankee Batboy - The Luckiest Kid in New York: The Anthony Florio Story.

The Neighborhood

In 1920, my father Sabato Florio was three years old when he and his parents left Naples, Italy, sailed on the SS Thomas and landed at Ellis Island; to be processed for entry into the United States. Their destination was affordable living quarters in Little Italy, arranged for them by relatives who had arrived the year before. As a young boy, my father occupied a lot of his time in his mother's kitchen and observed her as she would prepare the evening's meals – carefully cleaning vegetables, plucking feathers from fresh-killed chickens, scaling fresh fish and butchering large cuts of meat – watching as she would cook with the very best olive oil, fresh herbs and spices; herbs such as basil and oregano, grown in ceramic pots placed on a fire escape or on a building rooftop. My father also watched his father, like so many other fathers of the day, make bathtub gin and whiskey; something my father did not teach me. He was a good and observant student and within a few years became a very good cook himself, capable of preparing an entire meal for his mother and father. Through the early 1940s Sabato, known as Sal in the neighborhood, found work in the great bakeries in Little Italy, enabling him to employ the skills learned in Mama's kitchen.

Having met, falling in love with and marrying my mother, Rose Caputo, a beautiful young Calabrian immigrant, my father, at the time, wanted to open his own restaurant. In 1954 he did open his very first restaurant on Mott Street; *The King of Kings Pizza*. Notably, Mott Street became even more famous in 1972 in *The Godfather* when Vito Corleone (Marlon Brando) was shot several times as he walked from a fruit stand. In 1965, he would open *Florio's* in the heart of Little Italy, but for the time being, that opportunity would have to wait; while he worked as a driver for Johnson Motor Lines and saved for the day when he would start his own business. What could not wait, however, was the birth of their only child, and on November 3rd 1946, Sal and Rose Florio brought me into the world.

     We lived in a nice apartment at 384 Broome Street in the heart of Little Italy. The building, an impressive twenty-family brick and stone structure, is situated between two other famous streets, Mott and Mulberry. Broome Street was a main thoroughfare in the neighborhood and it was always alive with people, young and old, and like so many other kids in Little Italy, my first steps were out the door, down the stairs and onto the sidewalk. The general rule for younger neighborhood kids was that they could go outside, stay on the stoop, stay on the block, maybe go around the corner, but they could not cross the street unless they got permission from their mother, father or neighborhood guardian. A guardian could be a friend's parent, a store owner or even a regular street vendor.

I was a good kid, not a saint, but a pretty good kid. I obeyed my parents, respected the older folks in the neighborhood – if not, word would get back to my parents and there'd be hell to pay – and I got along with all of the other kids in the neighborhood, and growing up in Little Italy was one of the greatest experiences in my life; to this day I cherish the memories of those wonderful times. 384 Broome Street had a life of its own and was filled with immigrant families from Europe and Scandinavia, and it was also filled with music, often blaring out of each apartment's open doors and windows, and in the early afternoon, from the tiny kitchens in each apartment, the incredible aroma of, for the most part, Italian cooking being prepared for that evening's supper would be inhaled while walking up and down the stairwells. Outside of the rear windows of each apartment or communal hallway, freshly washed linens and clothes would be hung to dry, attached to clotheslines with wooden clothespins; clotheslines stretching across to a neighboring building, the wash blowing in the breeze that passed through the back alleys behind the buildings.

Shopping for the evening meal was an easy, affordable and enjoyable chore for my mother and for her neighbors. She walked down a few flights of stairs, out of the building and within one block, could buy the freshest fruits and vegetables at *Caruso's* on Mott Street, fresh meat cut by the butcher at *DiSantis,* freshly ground coffee, the absolutely very best bread in New York City at *Parisi Bakery* and, on special occasions, pastries or cookies from *Ferrara* or *Café*

Roma; the freshest mozzarella and other Italian foods from *Alleva* and from *DiPalo's*. And this could be done every day and usually was. Apartment kitchens were small and not accommodating to bags of groceries and sundry items, and why wouldn't someone choose to buy the freshest ingredients if they could get them a few feet from their doorstep.

Life at 384 Broome Street was a great experience and living there taught me the fundamental principles of human activity – love, respect, awareness, knowledge, relationship to others – and it is also where I developed the street-smarts that have influenced my life to this day. An only child, I loved my parents and loved living in the warm and comfortable apartment on Broome Street, but like so many young apartment dwellers in Little Italy, I loved being outside of the apartment even more so. Kids in the late 1940s and early 1950s had plenty of ways to occupy their time at home; homework, reading, writing, record players, radios and maybe even a small black and white television set, if they were lucky, but we did not have today's modern technology; I-Pads, computers, computer games, the internet, Facebook, Twitter cell phones, DVDs, CDs or I-Phones. We did have a record player in our apartment, and I did buy 45s at Rossi's Italian Novelty store for a quarter, so I did have something to listen to other than the radio. When I got bored with apartment life and really needed something better to do, I would just go outside. For me and my friends, the streets of Little Italy were our playground, offering lots of choices for neighborhood kids. Summertime offered the greatest variety and also the most fun for us kids. Fire hydrants were turned into sprinklers by placing wooden barrels with holes drilled into the sides, over the hydrants, turning Broome Street and Mott Street into a water park. The roofs became *tar beach* and were the neighborhood's sun-decks and tanning salons.   On very hot and humid days a few of us would run a hose up to the roof, to spray each other and cool off. Ball-playing of every description was my favorite choice – kick the can, stoop-ball, punch-ball and of course, stickball – and I would play in the streets from sunrise to sunset. When I wasn't playing ball I was talking about playing ball, and when I wasn't talking about playing ball I would listen to a ballgame on the radio, and when I went to sleep I would dream about playing ball; when I woke up the next morning, it would start all over again.

Before the playing would begin, or later on, after a dozen games or so, I would often walk to 158 Mott Street to visit my grandmother, Lucy Caputo.   To ever have known one's grandparents and to have shared a warm and loving relationship with them is for most cultures, a very unique and cherished experience. For Italian-Americans in Little Italy in the 1950s and 1960's, having grandparents living in the same neighborhood, a block or two away from my own doorstep, was not necessarily unique, but it was most definitely cherished. Grandma was a widow who lived by herself in a small apartment on Mott Street and always enjoyed, if not expected regular visits from her grandson.   To keep her company, she also had a cat in the apartment. One holiday, in preparation for the

Christmas Eve dinner, grandma had been soaking *baccala*–a pungent fish commonly sold in a dry form by the local fish monger – in a large pot of water that was placed on top of the refrigerator, out of the reach of the cat, she thought. She left the apartment for a few minutes to buy some more fresh ingredients, assuming everything would be fine in her absence. Though the fish may have been out of the immediate reach of the cat, its aroma wafted through the small apartment and was detected by the keen olfactory senses of her cat, so onto the counter it leaped and up to the top of the refrigerator it sprang. When grandma returned to the apartment she noticed that her cat was somewhat sleepy, meowing in an unusual and unfamiliar way. Suspecting the worst, she raced into the kitchen and reached up to inspect her pot. Three pounds of well-soaked pungent baccala had been consumed. For the remainder of that Christmas Season and for all the other Christmases to follow, my grandmother would live by herself in her apartment on Mott Street, without the company of a cat.

Living in New York City, right through the late 1950s was for baseball lovers, a great period in baseball history, because New York City had three professional teams; the Brooklyn Dodgers, the New York Giants and the New York Yankees. Each team had its own army of fans whose love for their team's heroes was passionate and unconditional. For me there was only one professional baseball team in New York City, or in any other city in the United States for that matter. For me and for a few close neighborhood friends, the New York Yankees were more than a team to be revered and idolized; more than the best team that ever played. For me the New York Yankees were a religion, a nation, a continent and a planet. Every conversation about any topic during and after baseball season was about the New York Yankees. I loved to tease my cousin Ernie about how much better a team the Yankees were, compared to the Brooklyn Dodgers. Ernie was a few years older, lived in Brooklyn and was a die-hard Dodger fan. In 1955 however, Ernie would have his revenge when the Brooklyn Dodgers defeated the New York Yankees in the seventh and decisive game of the 1955 World Series. I tried to avoid Ernie for weeks after. For so many Brooklynites, 1955 was the year when the world began.

At 384 Broome Street I was not the only family member who loved the game of baseball. My father's position with Johnson Motor Lines afforded him flexible hours, enabling him to indulge his love and his interest in baseball and to coach sandlot teams. Starting in Manhattan, at 54th Street on the West Side, his team, the DeMaro-Falcones – named after two neighborhood heroes killed during World War II – was part of the New York Federation League (NYFL) The NYFL teams were sponsored by the Journal American Newspaper; playing against each other throughout the other Boroughs in the City. The field on 54th Street was more rock than sand, still, under those conditions my father did a very good job coaching the team and improving his players' skills in Manhattan; so he took the team to the Bronx to play against a few of the City's better teams. While playing there he noticed and made it a point to remember, that the teams in the Bronx were much better than the Manhattan teams, and he was eventually persuaded by the manager of one of the teams to become the coach for one of the Bronx teams; *The New York Redwings*. All of the teams in the league were categorized by the players' ages, and the Redwings had a freshman, junior and senior division.

One of the players for the Freshman Redwings was me, a capable pitcher with a good fastball, and I also played infield and outfield. Each year after, I graduated to the next division; finally reaching the senior division. My favorite experience as pitcher came one sunny afternoon in the Bronx as I faced a future Hall of Famer, Rod Carew at the plate. With Major League scouts present at the game that day, there to take a good look at the talents of Rod Carew, and after two mediocre pitches, I fired one of my very best inside fastballs, forcing Carew to ground out to second base. I felt great after that pitch, at least until the next few batters came to the plate. As I recall they hit me all over the outfield, infield and every other field until my father signaled for the relief pitcher.

My father did a really good job as the coach of the New York Redwings and built a team with a few very good ballplayers, and baseball fans throughout the City would often tell him about promising players in other Boroughs; suggesting that he should check them out. A number of scouts for the professional teams had also heard about my father, and scouts for the White Sox and for the Cardinals tried to sign a few of his better players for their respective teams.   In one game for the NYFL City Championship, the Redwings were pitted against a great team from Gravesend, Brooklyn known as the *Brooklyn Cadets.* The game took place at the Parade Grounds in Brooklyn and was played in front of a large crowd of baseball fans. The teams were evenly matched and the score remained tied for most of the game, until a big Brooklyn kid named Joe Torre stepped up to the plate and hit the game-winning home run for the Cadets. Joe was the classic Brooklyn kid; he didn't talk a lot about doing stuff, he just stepped up to the plate and crushed the ball.

As a direct result of my father's coaching skills for the Redwings, more than thirty of his players were signed to contracts with farm teams for the Major Leagues, including Ed Kranepool, who went on to play for the New York Mets, Duke Carmel who played for the New York Mets, the New York Yankees and the St. Louis Cardinals, and Ken Singleton, who went on to play for the Montreal Expos, the Baltimore Orioles and the New York Mets. In my opinion, Ken Singleton was the best ballplayer to have ever played on my father's team. After retiring from Major League baseball, Ken Singleton continued to play a role in his favorite sport by becoming a radio and TV announcer and is, today, an announcer for the New York Yankees. I think my father did a pretty good job with all of the ballplayers he coached.

In The Bronx

My father loved the game of baseball and everything to do with it, and like so many other Italian-Americans, became attracted to the sport because of Joe DiMaggio. Sure, Babe Ruth was great and Lou Gehrig was incredible, but Joe DiMaggio was a *paesano* and my father could not be any prouder than to claim Joe D. as one of his own. On one very rare occasion in the early 1950s, Dad had an opportunity to see his favorite baseball player in person. Word had buzzed around the neighborhood that Joe DiMaggio and Marilyn Monroe were dining at *Villa Penza*, one of the great restaurants in Little Italy at that time. My father raced home, scooped me up in his arms and he, my mother and I ran down the street to the restaurant, just to say hello to the famous couple – the world famous ballplayer and the most famous, most beautiful movie star, right in their own neighborhood. Years later, in the very same neighborhood, I would cross paths again with Joe DiMaggio as well as with another famous and beautiful movie star.

My father wanted the best for me and tried to keep me on the straight and narrow. While I might have attended the neighborhood Catholic School, but for the strict academic requirements, I fared much better in the public school system and did my best while attending PS 130. In 1961, however, I would be headed for high school and my father had serious reservations about sending me to a Manhattan public high school. Some schools in Manhattan were rated very well, but in 1961, because of travelling restrictions, a student could only attend the high school in his district and my father just could not see me attending the school nearest to Little Italy.

One of the scouts who always came to the Redwings' games in the Bronx was a great guy named Steve Ray; a scout for the Chicago White Sox. In addition to his role as baseball scout Steve Ray was also the Athletic Director of James Monroe High School – in the Bronx. Having known each other from the Redwings' games, my father and Steve Ray became reacquainted. My father wanted to see a better player in me than I actually was and he would try just about anything to improve my chances, so he approached Steve Ray with a proposition; to get me into James Monroe High School in the Bronx

Attending a New York City public high school in one Borough while residing in another Borough was not permitted; in fact it was not legal. Steve Ray was a good man and would have no part in breaking any rules, so my father had to come up with a better plan. Though my father's primary objective was to help me to get into a school with an academic rating higher than the schools in Little Italy he also wanted me to get into James Monroe because the school had the best baseball team in New York City, *The Monroe Eagles*; a better plan was being formed in my father's head. One of the players on the Redwings was a kid named Paul who lived at 1142

Metcalf Avenue in the Bronx. Committed to his plan, my father approached Paul and asked him if I could use his Bronx address so that I could register at James Monroe; also insisting that Paul get his parents' approval to do so. Interestingly, Paul's parents did agree, so the stage was set, the die was cast and in September of 1961, I, a Manhattan resident, would soon be attending James Monroe High School, in the Bronx.

While at school, I made an honest attempt to show my gratitude to my father and to Steve Ray for getting me into James Monroe, by getting to class on time, by trying my best academically and, generally, by staying out of trouble. In my father's eyes however, the greatest demonstration of my gratitude was evidenced in my trying out, as a freshman, for the varsity baseball team and by making the team. Though I had made the team as a freshman I did not get a chance to play for the Eagles because, even though I made the team, the Juniors and Seniors at James Monroe High School were extremely good and it would be some time before I might have a chance to play.

Aside from playing the bench for the Eagles, things were going pretty well for me and I was grateful for my good luck and for the situation in which I found myself. One afternoon between classes I wandered into the gym to say hello to Steve Ray. I would often stop in to say hello to Mr. Ray to talk about school, the team and of course, the Yankees. Steve Ray was a scout for the Chicago White Sox but, unknown to me and my friends, because he had access to so many available students, Steve Ray was also on regular assignment for the New York Yankees; as a supplier of team ball-boys and batboys. In this role, he was able to observe potential candidates and to determine whether or not they had the mental attitude necessary for the position, as well as the right character to handle the task.

During our chat, Steve Ray dropped into the conversation that he had received a call from someone at Yankee Stadium that morning. Just the mention of Yankee Stadium stirred my curiosity, causing me to move closer to the edge of the standard issue, Board of Education wood and metal chair upon which I sat. "Mr. Ray, did you just say that someone from Yankee Stadium actually called you this morning?" I asked. "Yup." He answered. "Well why did they call and what did they want?" I asked impatiently. As I tried to sit still, Steve Ray explained that in the coming season the ball-boys assigned to the visiting teams at Yankee Stadium in 1961 would be moving on, and that the Stadium would need two new ball-boys to assist in the visiting dugout. "So Anthony, would you be interested in going up to Yankee Stadium to apply for a position for the visiting teams?" he asked. Ever the wiseass, I replied, "Well, I don't know. I've been pretty busy lately, and.....are you kidding me?" "Who do I have to see?" "Where do I have to go" "What do I have to do?" Mr. Ray gave me a slip of paper with all of the necessary details written on it and told me when to go to Yankee Stadium. "Tell them who you are and that I sent you."

I would need to report to the manager of the visitors' clubhouse, a great guy named Mickey Rendine, who would determine if I and one other boy were clubhouse material.

The very next afternoon after my last class at James Monroe, I hopped on the train and seemed to float for the entire ride to Yankee Stadium. I got off the train, ran down the steps and flew to the Stadium. Stopping at a security booth to ask how to find Mr. Rendine, I tried to corral all of the thoughts swirling around in my head; where I was, who I was about to see, what I might be doing and the chance that I might actually meet a New York Yankee; that I might actually meet Mickey Mantle – very heavy thinking for a skinny fifteen year old kid from Manhattan who ate, slept and drank baseball.

"Kid; hey kid!" the security guard said in a loud voice jarring me out of my daydream. "Here's a pass for you to go down to the visitor's clubhouse. Mr. Rendine is waiting for you." Walking into Yankee Stadium for the first time in my life, in the very same underground tunnels that Babe Ruth had walked through, I held my breath as I looked and stared and gawked at every inch of this incredible ballpark. Some force seemed to guide me towards the visitor's clubhouse because, to this day, I don't know how I got there. "Over here kid." called Mickey Rendine as I kept staring into space. Mickey Rendine was about thirty five years old, was in pretty good shape and had a welcoming grin for me and for the two other kids who also came to the Stadium to be interviewed. Mr. Rendine was a native of the Bronx and was a fixture at Yankee Stadium. After a relatively brief interview about their background and an explanation of what their responsibilities would be in the clubhouse, Fred Williamson and I were selected as the new ball-boys who would be assigned to the first base and third base lines in Yankee Stadium in the spring of 1962.

As I rode the train back to Little Italy, the other passengers stared at this skinny kid who just kept smiling and muttering to himself, shaking his head in disbelief. I couldn't wait to tell my parents, and anyone and everyone in the neighborhood and at James Monroe High School and anywhere and everywhere I found myself. I couldn't wait to tell and to thank Steve Ray. But of all the things that I could not wait for, the one thing that I absolutely hated having to wait for was the spring of 1962.

The Visitor's Clubhouse

Steve Ray was genuinely happy for the good fortune of my being chosen as ball-boy at Yankee Stadium for the coming season and continued to be a good friend to my father and a positive force in my life. In keeping with his interest in my welfare, Steve was instrumental in helping to juggle my classroom schedule as the baseball season approached. Mickey Rendine was a nice guy but if I wanted to remain in his good graces, I would need to get to the clubhouse at least three hours before the start of each game. So throughout the spring of 1962 at James Monroe High School my schedule did not include gym and did not include lunch, enabling me to reach the clubhouse, hungry, but with time to spare.

As April 1962 approached, I became extremely anxious and was constantly distracted by thoughts of going to Yankee Stadium. For anyone who has ever hoped for a chance to realize a dream, or who may have ever obsessed over an imagined encounter with a favorite celebrity or famous sports legend, realizing that dream or actually meeting that famous person could make a person's life complete. For me, a fifteen year old street-wise kid from Little Italy who until attending James Monroe High School, rarely went anywhere outside of the neighborhood, a kid not given to long stories about his daily routine or family life; for me no words could be found to describe how I felt inside about going to Yankee Stadium. To be with professional ballplayers in their clubhouse and in the dugout; to be so close to the field; to smell the grass and the pine tar and the beer; to hear the loud crack of the bat; to see so many famous people; almost too much for such a young man to comprehend. Every day leading up to opening day, my head ached, my ears rang, my heart pounded and my thoughts just drifted into space.

Before opening day, I met with Mickey Rendine at the visitor's clubhouse to learn the lay of the land. The general rule of thumb was not to bother the players and to try to stay out of their way. The more routine responsibilities for the visiting team's ball-boys would include cleaning spikes, picking up after the players, bringing towels to the laundry-room and basically, doing what anyone in the clubhouse told you to do. The visitor's clubhouse itself was pretty empty; just enough lockers for the team, a black & white TV and one large shower stall with several shower-heads.

I was in the visiting clubhouse especially early on April 10, 1962. I tended to my responsibilities with great purpose and skill, cleaning as best I could and readying the lockers for the visiting team. April 10, 1962 was opening day at Yankee Stadium and the visiting team, the first professional ballplayers who I would ever meet up close and personal, would be the Baltimore Orioles. The Orioles were a very good team and had signed a number of famous players to their roster, and my very first game as ball-boy would be a memorable one.

In they came, like gladiators to the *Coliseum,* like gods from the heavens; professional baseball players marching into the clubhouse, one by one. Professional baseball players! I tried to move but I couldn't · Brooks Robinson, Whitey Herzog, Hoyt Wilhelm, Dave McNally, Marv Throneberry, Boog Powell – I tried to act normal but I could not; I just stared, eyes wide open, as I leaned against the nearest wall. In they came, talking, laughing, smoking; changing from street clothes to Oriole uniforms.

I was a die-hard Yankee fan but I did know a little about their competitors. Brooks Robinson was right up there with Clete Boyer; the *Human Vacuum Cleaner* was Robinson's nickname and he was no pushover at third base. He was left-handed but he batted and threw right-handed. I had to admit that it was going to be great to watch the Yankees test Brooks' talents on the field on my first day at the Stadium. Boog Powell would be another guy to keep an eye on in left field, on first base, as well as at bat. He was a powerful hitter and could be a threat on a good day. Whitey Herzog had originally signed with the Yankees under Casey Stengel and was now a capable outfielder for Baltimore.

Earl Weaver was the Orioles Manager and would be as much fun to watch as his players. Only about 5' 4", Weaver was a tough little guy, well-respected and even feared by the team; no one wanted to get on his wrong side. He was short but not short on temper; often arguing with umpires over a bad call and running onto the field, spinning his hat around during his encounters with the umps.

As the Orioles left the clubhouse to go into dugout and onto the field, I followed closely behind, still mesmerized by my first experience of meeting a professional baseball team. I could not resist the urge to see a dugout from the inside and the first chance I had, I went in to see what it was like. I looked around for a moment but became immediately distracted by the activity on the field, in front of the dugout. The Orioles were warming up for the game, the fans were beginning to pour into the stands, batting practice was in full swing, and then I noticed the pinstripes.

As a ball-boy or batboy for a visiting team, it was important to show some form of solidarity with that team, some loyalty, some respect, regardless of my own preferences for the opposing team. From childhood I was always respectful to adults, in my family or in the neighborhood and would remain respectful to the somewhat older ballplayers on the Baltimore Orioles or on any of the other teams who would visit Yankee Stadium in 1962. But for as long as I could remember, the New York Yankees were as much a part of my life, if only from afar, as were my mother and father, and any attempt to control my enthusiasm would be as unnatural as for me as trying not to breathe.

I looked for him among the pinstripes. I stared at all of the numbers, craning my neck and straining my eyes; searching, waiting for him to appear. Then, through a crowd of players, umpires and newspaper reporters I spotted him; Number 7. Mickey Mantle. *Mickey Mantle*! He seemed to walk in slow motion, lumbering across the field like some giant being. I appeared calm, almost frozen, but for the perspiration beading on my forehead and dripping down my face. Inside my head, however, my voice was screaming. "Holy shit! It's him! Right here, right in front of my eyes! Holy shit!" "Thank you God, thank you Mr. Ray, thank you mom and dad for bringing me to life!" I didn't approach the Yankee players but I got as close as I could without drawing attention. For me that day, God was in His heaven and all was right with the world.

My first day as ball-boy for the visiting Baltimore Orioles was filled with excitement and adventure. I silently rooted for the Yankees and could not believe that my dream-team was playing, just a few feet from mine. As ball-boy, I was positioned along the first base line, and when an Orioles' player would get a hit or make an impressive defensive play I absolutely hated it. I loved the sport of baseball so much that, regardless of the outcome, the game itself was equally fulfilling, and any game that would include the New York Yankees would just be that much more fulfilling.

The Yankees won the opener, squeaking by Baltimore by one run with a score of 7 to 6, and though I was already on Cloud Nine, I was treated to one more thrill that afternoon. Mickey Mantle, batting lefty, smashed a line drive home run that just rocketed into the right centerfield bleachers, landing more than 425' from home plate. I would see other Mickey Mantle home runs in the next three years and would have a chance to get to know my idol better, but I would never forget the sound of that bat hitting that ball on that afternoon for the rest of my life.

The Visiting Teams

Being associated with Yankee Stadium, even being a ball-boy, had given me a kind of celebrity status in the neighborhood but my very best friends, Frank "Pizzi" Pizzimenti and Sal "Junior" Gondolfo, knew that I loved playing ball and loved talking about playing ball and loved the New York Yankees, so this experience with the visiting teams was just a natural evolution for their friend and they did not detect any increase in the size of my head. I talked continually with my friends about being at the game and seeing all those famous players, and about the games and players that I would be seeing throughout the season.

The next series of home games started on April 21st and the visiting team was the Cleveland Indians. I was on time for my job as ball-boy and the thrill of seeing professional ballplayers was still fresh in my mind. Eleven days had passed since the opener against Baltimore as I went about my chores in the clubhouse. Having had that first experience of meeting famous ballplayers, and having become more confident, I was a bit less anxious as I prepared to greet the Indians. Mudcat Grant, Doc Edwards and Johnny Romano entered the clubhouse and I introduced myself. James "Mudcat" Grant was a great pitcher for Cleveland and it was a real thrill to shake his big hand. Johnny Romano, a native of New Jersey, was one of the best catchers in his time and was having a good year in 1962.

Other players followed and once again I greeted Ken Aspromonte, Tito Francona and Tommy Agee. Ken Aspromonte was a Brooklyn native and though he played for Cleveland, he had New York written all over him. For the next two days I watched the Indians and the Yankees battle it out on the field; the Indians taking the opener and the Yankees winning the second game. I knew when to say something to the visiting team and when to remain silent. The Indians, like the Orioles before them, and like all the visiting teams after them, liked me and the players had no trouble autographing a ball or signing a program for such a nice kid.

As the season progressed I continued to do a good job in the visiting clubhouse, easily winning Mickey Rendine's approval and admiration, and I also did a pretty good job in getting to know the visiting teams. Always anxious about meeting the next visiting team and always in awe of the game's greats, my 1962 season as ball-boy was filled with one memorable encounter after the other. When Chicago came to town I was thrilled to meet White Sox greats Early Wynn, Luis Aparicio and Nellie Fox. Boston's Carl Yastrzemski was a favorite; Harmon Killebrew, Tony Oliva and Bob Allison of the Minnesota Twins stand out in my memory; Gino Cimoli of the Kansas City Athletics and Rocky Colavito of the Detroit Tigers. Norm Cash and Al Kaline, two other Detroit Tigers, were also memorable characters, but Norm cash is memorable for a different reason. Norm Cash always seemed to be angry, always seemed to have a chip on his shoulder and came across

as a tough guy. *Stormin Norman* to his fans and
teammates, was born in Texas and entered sports as a
football player; as a running back for the Chicago Bears.
To me he looked like *Butch* of the *Little Rascals*, and
during the three series in May, June and August of 1962
in which the Tigers were guests of Yankee Stadium,
Norm Cash was an intimidating character. Wise beyond
my fifteen years, I figured that Norm Cash, having
grown up in Texas, was just not comfortable in big cities,
surrounded by thousands of New Yorkers. That's how I
perceived him, anyway. Maybe in his case perception
was reality.

Ryne Duren, Jim Fregosi and Joe Koppe of the
Los Angeles Angels were pretty good guys as well and I
came to know Joe Koppe on a more personal level. Joe
Koppe, an infielder for the Angels, was born in Detroit
and was in pretty good shape; an exercise freak as I
recall. Joe took a liking to me and one afternoon after
the game, joked about my exercising regimen and
challenged me to do some sit-ups. "I'll give you five
bucks if you can do fifty sit-ups in sixty seconds!" said
Joe. In 1962 five dollars for a minute's worth of work
was a lot of money, so I accepted the challenge gladly.
To Joe Koppe's amazement, I did fifty five sit-ups in
sixty seconds, and he was happy to give me the five
dollar bill. "What else have you got?" I said, now
challenging Joe Koppe. His next exercise would
challenge me to do one very difficult Japanese-style
push-up, which required the skills of an acrobatic
contortionist. I was able to do five push-ups in the

allotted sixty seconds, and Joe gave me another five dollar bill. "Ten bucks for two minute's work! Wow!" Joe received a lot of ribbing from all of the guys in the locker room that day; how this skinny kid got over on him because I was in better shape than Joe ever thought. They never let up, and Joe had to finally leave the locker room to get away from all the noise. This was going to be a good day for me.

When the Washington Senators came to town I was given an opportunity to see a darker side of human nature. Jimmy Piersall, the great centerfielder for the Senators, was an outstanding ballplayer, often compared to Joe DiMaggio, and was a very likable guy. Jimmy was an East Coast guy, born in Connecticut, and was one of the best centerfielders of his time. His antics on the field would always thrill the fans and when he was in the right frame of mind, Jimmy could be a very funny guy. During one game, having reached first on a base hit, Piersall took a lead toward second while Yankee-great Bill Stafford was on the mound. Stafford fired to first, but Jimmy got back in time. This continued as Stafford threw to first three more times. As he took his next lead toward second, Jimmy pretended to hold a camera and then pretended to film Bill Stafford as he pitched to the next batter. The crowd enjoyed the pantomime but Stafford was not amused. In another game at the Stadium, as the Senators took the field Jimmy ran to the monuments in the outfield and ducked down behind them, pretending that no one could see him. In the 1960s there were actually three stone monuments placed out in deep centerfield dedicated to three of the greatest Yankees who were ever in the game; Miller Huggins, dedicated in 1932 in the center, Lou Gehrig, dedicated in 1941 on the left, and Babe Ruth, dedicated in 1949 on the right. The joking around caused the inning to be delayed and again the fans roared at Jimmy's antics. When he was not in the right frame of mind, however, Jimmy Piersall's personality would darken and he would become depressed and emotionally unbalanced. Before meeting Jimmy Piersall I had never met anyone with such a severe mental condition and though it was hard for a fifteen year old kid to process, I learned an important lesson in how well someone can survive when faced with such serious challenges. In Piersall's biographies, *Fear Strikes Out* and *The Truth Hurts,* his mental condition, diagnosed as bipolar disorder, would later explain the cause of his antics and mood swings on the field, but his capabilities as a professional ballplayer remain respected and admired, especially by me.

The Yankees had a great year in 1962, winning the Pennant and reinforcing the strength of their legacy. For me this achievement meant only one thing; I would be attending every game of the 1962 World Series at Yankee Stadium. For Mickey Rendine the World Series was a major event but for me it was everything. The visiting team clubhouse may not have looked any different but it most certainly felt different; the clubhouse was about to be occupied by the *National League's Pennant* winners, the San Francisco Giants, and I addressed every chore with great excitement and enthusiasm. What an incredible opportunity for a young baseball fan; to be in the clubhouse during the World Series and to be able to meet famous ballplayers. Though I was never a New York Giants fan, along with millions of other New York baseball fans, I was upset by the loss of both the New York Giants and the Brooklyn Dodgers at the end of the 1957 season – both teams had decided to leave New York and moved to California – so having a chance to see one former New York team play against the current New York team would be fantastic. It also afforded me an opportunity to meet the great Willy Mays; probably one of the nicest guys I ever met in my life. Willy Mays was a gentle, soft spoken man, who made me feel very special; just by speaking with me and seeming to take a genuine interest in my role in the clubhouse. Willy Mays was born in Westfield, Alabama and not unlike Mickey Mantle, was introduced to the sport of baseball by his father. At the age of ten, Willy was being groomed and trained to become one of the greatest ballplayers in the history of the game.

While the players, fans and promoters were preparing for professional baseball's main event another very serious, very frightening event was unfolding outside of the world of sports; an event that had captured the attention of everyone else in the world. In September of 1962, while engaging in routine reconnaissance flights over Cuba, American spy-planes discovered and photographed evidence of missile bases under construction; Russian missiles armed with nuclear warheads were identified in a number of photographs and it was determined that a *clear and present danger* existed, 90 miles from the coastline of the United States. Clearly viewed as an overtly hostile action on the part of the Soviet Union in league with Castro's Cuba, President Kennedy appeared on television and informed the citizens of the United States that the threat was real and that he would do everything in his power to defend the Nation, including the very real possibility of attacking Cuba preemptively. Russia's actions had gone far beyond saber rattling and the Soviet leader, Nikita Khrushchev was the perfect bad-guy to have in control of the launch codes. Kennedy ordered a naval blockade, preventing additional ships carrying deadly cargo from reaching Cuba. By October 8, 1962, *Black Saturday*, the rhetoric had reached a fevered pitch and most Americans believed that a nuclear war with Russia was imminent. American flags hung from windows, doors and rooftops across the country; signs claiming *Better Dead than Red* were seen everywhere; houses of worship were packed with people preparing to meet their maker.

By October 28, 1962, miraculously and thankfully, the crisis was averted, but history has revealed some sobering facts about the *Cuban Missile Crisis*. If not for the counseling of Attorney General Robert Kennedy, who convinced his brother John to seek a diplomatic resolution to the crisis by secretly agreeing to remove American missiles from Turkey – an action not made public to the American people until years after their removal – Khrushchev, as he stated years later in an interview in 1982, would have launched Soviet ICBMs armed with nuclear warheads into the cities of NATO members around the world. If ever a distraction to world events in 1962 was in order, the World Series was definitely it.

The first World Series game of my life was played at Yankee Stadium on October 7, 1962. This was the third game of the series, and the visiting Giants would be arriving after having evened the series by winning the second game in San Francisco and shutting out the Yankees 2-0. And so, to my great joy, the National League Champion San Francisco Giants entered the visiting team's clubhouse on that brisk October afternoon. The great pitchers, Juan Marichal, Gaylord Perry and Don Larsen, who once pitched for the Yankees; infielder Orlando Cepeda; great outfielders Filipe Alou, Willie McCovey, Harvey Kuenn and Manny Mota, entering, smiling with confidence. When I saw Willie Mays play, even the biggest Mickey Mantle fan would agree that Mays was one of the best to ever play in the majors. But the thought running through my head was less than kind. Under my breath I said "If he's so good then let's see what he's got, playing against Mickey Mantle!"

The three World Series games at Yankee Stadium in 1962 were the icing on the cake for an already unbelievable year and I never took my good fortune for granted, always thanking the heavens after each new encounter or introduction. The opening Game Three would see the Yankees take the lead in the series so I kept a low profile in the clubhouse after the game. Game Four would be evened up by the Giants, and in a record-setting way. With the game tied at 2-2 Chuck Hiller, a mediocre player with few home runs to speak of came to the plate with the bases loaded. Marshall Bridges, a strong left-hander with a pretty good fastball, was on the mound for New York and did not perceive Hiller as a threat, so he hurled what he believed to be an unhittable fastball towards the plate. For the first time in World Series history, with the bases loaded, a National League player sent a fastball, or any other ball for that matter, into the stands, scoring the very first Grand Slam home run for the league, also enabling San Francisco to win Game Four and tie up the series. I was a witness to baseball history that day and recorded the event in my memory. I can't say that I didn't know it or feel it at the time, but how incredibly lucky was I to have been present that day? I have never forgotten those great memories.

Spirits were much higher in the visitor's clubhouse after Game Four and I may have acted interested, but I hated the fact that the Yankees had lost. Any opposing team was the enemy and I felt that I had betrayed my favorite team by being remotely associated with the Giants.

The Yankees would win game five in New York and then travel to Candlestick Park to win the 1962

World Series in Game Seven. My season as ball-boy for the visiting teams at Yankee Stadium, concluding with an on-the-field view of three World Series games, could not have been more memorable for a fifteen year old baseball fan; a behind the scenes look at famous ballplayers, dozens of autographs and souvenirs, watching every New York Yankee game at Yankee Stadium in person and a chance to see Mickey Mantle play ball right in front of my eyes. It would be hard for me to imagine any time or anything ever even coming close to 1962.

Spring 1963

On November 3, 1962 I turned sixteen
and, as far as I was concerned, all of my birthday and
Christmas presents were paid in full for the next fifty
years. The world, having stepped back from the brink of
nuclear war, was at peace for now, and what trinket
could possibly ever match the gift of being part of
Yankee Stadium, working with famous ballplayers and
watching the New York Yankees play ball for an entire
baseball season? No, I was not an ungrateful child and
the wonderful memories of those experiences in the
spring and summer of 1962 would, I truly believed,
sustain me for a lifetime. But in the coming spring of
1963 the luckiest kid in New York was about to become
a little bit luckier.

Returning home from school one afternoon in
March, my mother told me that someone had called for
me; someone from Yankee Stadium named Pete. I asked
her a million questions, but she just said to call him
back and find out what he wanted. I kind of just froze,
but I called the man back immediately, listened
carefully to each syllable and was told to come to the
Stadium tomorrow afternoon after school; no particular
reason was given, just to show up. A million thoughts
ran through my head as I tried to imagine the purpose of
the request; had I messed up in the visiting clubhouse;
did I take something I shouldn't have; could it be
possible that I might have another season with the
visiting teams as

batboy. Nothing seemed to satisfy my curiosity so I
tried to put the thought out of my head until the next
day; trying to sleep would be impossible; trying to
concentrate in the classrooms the next day was
impossible. When the bell rang, signaling the end of my
last period, I shot out of my seat, flew out of the doors of
James Monroe, ran to the train, got on and did not sit
down for the ride to the Stadium.

Running to the Stadium, I looked for the nearest
security guard and asked where I could find *Big Pete.*
"Why?" asked the guard in an annoyed tone. I explained
why I was there and was directed toward the Yankee
Clubhouse. "Over here kid." I heard in the distance in
an underground tunnel. As a ball-boy for the visiting
teams the year before, I had a chance to visit the Yankee
clubhouse while running errands for Mickey Rendine. I
did meet Big Pete last season but never had a chance to
say much to him. Pete Sheehy had been the equipment
manager for the Yankees since 1927 and was a fixture
at the Stadium; the "*keeper of the pinstripes*" as he was
often referred to. He was also a keeper of secrets and as
I would come to realize, never shared any of his
observations with anyone.

Big Pete explained that Mickey Rendine had been
very impressed with me throughout the 1962 season;
always on time, always polite, always completing the
tasks at hand and very well-liked by all of the visiting
teams. He went on to explain why he had asked me to
come down to the clubhouse; to the New York Yankee
Clubhouse

at Yankee Stadium. The selection of batboys and ball-boys at the Stadium followed a certain protocol. Generally the batboy and ball-boy for the Yankees would change from season to season and the new kids for each position would move from their respective positions in the visiting dugout over to the Yankee dugout. It so happened that the visiting teams' batboy for last season was not going to be asked to move over to the Yankees' dugout in the new season, so with Mickey Rendine's glowing endorsement, and with my consent, Big Pete was going to assign the job of *New York Yankee Batboy* to me. I immediately went into shock. This could not be happening to me again. I already had the gift of a lifetime last season, just being in Yankee Stadium with all of my heroes. As batboy for the Yankees I would be in the clubhouse with Mickey Mantle before and after every game. I could talk to him and ask him questions; I could tell him just how much I admired him. Mickey Mantle, Roger Maris, Yogi Berra, Elston Howard, Whitey Ford, Clete Boyer, Tony Kubek, and Bobby Richardson; every game played in Yankee Stadium and I would be present at every one of them. I composed myself and kept saying "Thank you. Thank you very much Mr. Sheehy. Thanks very much."

Once again other passengers on a train watched a skinny, smiling kid as I sat staring into space, muttering sounds, mumbling words, giggling, fidgeting and thanking God for having been born. To this day I am still amazed at how blessed I was to have been invited into the incredible, private world of the greatest team in baseball history; to really get to meet and to know such famous people and to become a small part of their lives. When I got to the neighborhood I told my mother and father and a few friends the news, and within days, word spread like wildfire throughout Little Italy. As I walked around the neighborhood, strangers would point to me and approach me, congratulating me on my new success, and I really enjoyed this, milking my popularity for all it was worth. Maybe my head did feel a little bit bigger and maybe I felt as if everyone was staring at me as I strolled around the streets, but it was just how I felt inside, and it showed. April could not arrive soon enough.

Reporting to Big Pete a few days before opening day, I toured the Yankee clubhouse. Physically, it was about three times larger than the visitor's clubhouse; one huge room, plush carpeting, lockers, stools, one big shower stall and a color TV set, but this was the clubhouse where Babe Ruth changed from street clothes into pinstripes and joked with the other players; where Lou Gehrig kicked off his spikes; where Joe DiMaggio sat and spoke with reporters. This was the New York Yankees' clubhouse that housed *the Legends of sports history,* and almost from the beginning, Big Pete was part of that history. Yankee Stadium was only 4 years old when Pete Sheehy signed on as Equipment Manager with the Yankees in 1927. He watched Babe Ruth hit home runs and saw Lou Gehrig run the bases; he assigned a locker to Joe DiMaggio and he also assigned the *Number 7* to Mickey Mantle.

It was to Big Pete who Lou Gehrig handed his spikes when he had had enough of baseball and was forced to retire. Big Pete had already been an integral part of the New York Yankees organization for 36 years before I ever set foot in the New York Yankee clubhouse. When Pete came to Yankee Stadium the Yankee clubhouse was on the third base side of the field; the organization moved it to the first base side in 1946. The clubhouse itself was a large, rectangle shaped space with lockers running around the perimeter of the room. I learned that there was a kind of pecking order to how lockers were assigned to the players. The better players were given lockers that were further away from the door; almost secluded in a way.

Even today it's considered a privilege to have a locker that is as far away from the door as possible. I had a million questions for Big Pete but soon discovered that the answers to most of the questions would be locked away forever in Big Pete's very private memory; not to be discussed, disclosed or divulged. It was understood that what happened in the clubhouse stayed in the clubhouse. He also told me not to believe anything I hear and only half of what I see.

In the middle of the clubhouse stood a large table filled with about five dozen brand new baseballs, and before each game all of the players had to autograph balls, to be given to the owners, sponsors and friends. For one reason or another some of the players were not required to sign balls and instead of receiving a baseball signed by Mickey Mantle or by Whitey Ford, some unsuspecting sponsor very probably received a ball signed by *Little Pete* Previte, Big Pete's assistant. A few sponsors even received balls signed by yours truly; when Little Pete had too many balls to sign on his own.

Pete described what my duties as batboy would be in the dugout, but unlike those responsibilities in the visitor's clubhouse, I would not have any chores in the Yankee clubhouse; New York Yankee batboys were gods in their own right. Before each game I would bring all of the bats out to the dugout and place them in racks for each player to choose, and after a batter got on base or returned to the dugout I would pick up the bat and put it back in the rack. Pete also explained that in the dugout, Yankee third base Coach Frank Crosetti was in charge and that I would follow and obey all of Coach Crosetti's rules and regulations; no ifs ands or buts. Pete tended to some chores and I walked around the clubhouse on my own; in total awe and disbelief. "I just do not believe that I am here." I kept saying to myself.

I walked out of the clubhouse and up to the Yankee dugout; just to look around. As I stared onto the empty field I imagined the Yankees in their respective defensive positions; Joe Pepitone right in front of my eyes on first base, maybe hugging it for a powerful left-handed batter. At second I could see Bobby Richardson playing deep for a power-hitter. Tony Kubek was moving in and out and back and forth at shortstop, assessing the best position, preparing for the next batter. Third base would be covered, smothered even, by the incredible Clete Boyer, trapping anything that dared to pass him. Whitey Ford was on the mound throwing to

Yogi Berra or to Elston Howard; either man protecting the plate from would-be base stealers to home. I saw Roger Maris, shy and smiling in left field and Tom Tresh, punching his glove in right field. And then I imagined Mickey Mantle in centerfield, crouching, hands on knees ready to explode after a fly ball to the outfield. "Anthony!" called Big Pete. "Hey kid. C'mon!" I awoke from my daydream and ran to Pete. We went back to the clubhouse and I was directed to the space in which I would change into a batboy; through the clubhouse, past the showers into a private corner in the laundry-room. At that point I would have changed in the crawl-space under the clubhouse if I had to. Big Pete handed me a New York Yankee uniform. "Try it on kid. This is your new uniform." I just stared at it at first and kind of felt the weight of it; a New York Yankee pinstriped uniform. I put it on and looked in a big mirror on the wall. Maybe the hat was a bit large, but not so bad; but the uniform looked five sizes too big. I tucked in the shirt as far as it would go and then tightened the belt until I couldn't breathe. The stockings and socks were another challenge; a kind of two-part system. First I had to put on white socks, and then I had to step into the black, calf-length stockings that had stirrups on the bottom. I had to roll up the stockings three times to get them to fit right. The uniform was still too big. I laughed out loud, looking at myself in the mirror but stopped when I realized that I was in a New York Yankee uniform, standing in the clubhouse in Yankee Stadium, about to become the official batboy for the *World Champion New*

York Yankees. I just stared in the mirror as all these thoughts ran through my head.

The next day I went to see Steve Ray again, to tell him the incredible news. He was thrilled and just shook his head and smiled. Because of Steve Ray's influence my schedule remained the same as the year before, allowing me to get to the Stadium on time before the games; my new season was about to begin. The 1963 opener fell on April 11th and pitted the Yankees against the Baltimore Orioles. I had arrived at the clubhouse as early as possible that afternoon, immediately changed into my uniform and reported to Big Pete. "Okay kid, you're on. Just do what I told you and you'll be fine." All of the Yankees were already in the clubhouse and I walked over to introduce myself to Whitey Ford and Roger Maris and Clete Boyer, and then Mickey Mantle, larger than life, walked over to meet me. I tried to speak but I could not. I tried to move but nothing worked. Mickey Mantle may have said something to me but I still can't remember what he said. Then Mantle rubbed my cap and went back to his locker to change. "You okay kid?" asked Big Pete. "You look a little pale."

My very first encounter with Mickey Mantle was a memorable experience. Mickey was such a nice guy and was very approachable, though I did not go near him for a while; I just stepped back and watched my idol get ready for the game. When I noticed Mickey's legs for the first time I could not believe how they looked and how they needed to be bandaged and taped before each game. Unless you'd seen Mickey's legs up close, as I did, you would never know how hard it was for him to play as well as he did. This still boggles my mind when I think of him. Before and after most games he would soak in a whirlpool to relieve the swelling in his legs. Since then I've often wondered how today's technology or wonder-drugs might have helped him to be a healthier player. On occasion, a replacement runner would be sent in to relieve Mickey if necessary. A player named Jack Reed relieved Mickey on many occasions, including one game that lasted for 22 innings. In that long game Jack Reed, having replaced Mickey in center field, became the hero of the day when he hit a home run that finally won the game.

I believed that Mickey was an incredible athlete and was so powerful and could overcome anything. Mickey Mantle was 5'11" but in that first encounter I believed that he was seven feet tall.

I left the clubhouse following the Yankees; walking right behind the team to the Yankee dugout. As Pete had instructed, I reported to Frank Crosetti and introduced myself. Frank Crosetti was the Yankee third base coach and was well liked and respected by the team. Born in San Francisco, Crossetti came from a part of California that had produced a few other well-known Italian-American ballplayers; Tony Lazzeri, Charlie Silvera and a couple of DiMaggio brothers. He had joined the Yankee organization in 1932, was pretty good at shortstop and had a respectable batting average throughout his career; in 1946 he was assigned to third base as coach. Crosetti gave me a warm hello and said "Just do your job and be sure not to leave the dugout." but all I heard was that at no time, under any circumstances, for the entire season I could not go onto the field and had to stay in the dugout. Sitting with the New York Yankees in the dugout, watching them play within a few feet of the dugout was not necessarily a bad thing, but never leaving the dugout, other than to hand a bat to someone; this would have to change and I would be just the guy to fix that – just not on opening day on April 11, 1963.

As a few of the Yankees warmed up in front of the dugout I sat with the rest of the team, talking with one player after another in light conversation, but sitting in the dugout was pure torture and I had to figure out some way of getting onto the field. By the third game of the opening series with Baltimore, having proven to Frank Crosetti that I was a pretty good batboy and could be trusted to occasionally step out of the dugout, I climbed on top of the dugout to get a better look at the fans; especially the girl fans. I wanted to be noticed; I wanted everyone to know how lucky I was and I did a great job at attracting attention.

By the next series of games with the Detroit Tigers the reality had sunk in. Thrilled with being with my Yankee heroes, I also became more confident in my association with the players and with Frank Crosetti. After weeks of badgering and torturing and begging him, Crosetti relaxed some of his more rigid rules and permitted me to go onto the field; I attributed his concession to my employing the street smarts that I learned in Little Italy. My first big step out of the dugout and closer to the field was before the game, when I was permitted to have a catch with the players, but only in front of the dugout. I believe that this did not go unnoticed by the fans – though it probably did go unnoticed – as they watched me play. By the time the Minnesota Twins came to town on May 14, 1963, I had managed to go onto the field during batting practice to shag fly balls with the outfielders. This was just so unbelievably great for a young baseball fan; to be given a chance to be so close to these living legends, and the memories are vivid and the thrill is still there whenever I reminisce about my days at Yankee Stadium. And each time I go back to the Stadium to see the Yankees play, I stare into the outfield and still get the feeling I had when I was a skinny fifteen year old kid.

One of my favorite activities at the original Yankee Stadium was retrieving foul balls that had landed on top of the huge net behind home plate during the game. Greg Cahoon, a Yankee ball boy, and I were responsible for catching balls before they could hit the ground and could possibly hold-up the game. I would time my reaction so that the catch would appear to be that much more dramatic, often making spectacular one-handed catches to impress the crowd. This is when I earned the nickname *Hot Dog*, for showing off so well. As far as rating Hot Dogs goes, I would have to say that, overall, I ranked third out of the all-time greatest Hot Dogs; number one being Reggie Jackson, and Joe

Pepitone coming in at number two. Being a Hot Dog got me a lot of attention, which of course I loved. After every catch I would look into the stands to see if any pretty girls had watched me in action. One afternoon before the game, while having a catch with Johnny Blanchard, I turned to see if any of the girls were looking at me and Johnny hit me on the side of the head with a ball and I went down like a sack of potatoes. It hurt but I was okay, as a few Yankees ran over to check me out. "You okay kid?" someone asked as they picked me up. Rubbing my head and acting dazed I asked "Am I in the starting lineup?" So they knew I was okay and walked away laughing. As the season progressed I wanted to get even closer to the action, so I begged Crosetti for an opportunity to practice with the team in the infield. Maybe I was a bit too comfortable, maybe a bit cocky when I thought I'd give third base a try; big mistake! Stepping into the right-hand batter's box was the man himself; my idol, my hero – Mickey Mantle. Just ninety feet away from the skinny weasel from James Monroe High School stood Number 7. Mickey Mantle was extremely powerful; a block of pure muscle as everyone knows. A farm-boy from Oklahoma with powerful wrists and forearms, it would not be a stretch of the imagination to picture him carrying a pony or a bale of hay. He once told me that he built up his muscles and developed his great strength when he was a young boy, slinging a hammer every day in the coal mines. Mickey hit a number of balls into the outfield as well as a few towards second base. Just as I was becoming bored, Mantle crushed a line-drive within one

foot of my head. I heard the crack of the bat hitting the
ball and I felt the wind as something rocketed over me,
but I did not, could not see anything resembling a
baseball, nor would I have had a chance to reach for it if
I had seen something. By the time I got my glove up,
the ball was already in left field.   In all of my years as a
baseball fan, and to this day, I have never seen anyone
hit a ball as hard as Mickey Mantle.   Composing myself,
I thought I'd give short stop a try; deep short stop – a
much safer place to be. Crosetti let me practice with the
team because he knew that I could play ball and that I
would not be a danger to myself. Before the game
began, the starting lineup would take the field to warm
up as the coach hit balls to all of the players. As the
starting team players came off the field the back-up
team would replace them in different positions; I was
permitted to practice with the back-up team, did not
miss too many balls and felt very much like part of the
Yankees. It was during these practice sessions when I
felt like I was almost somebody; as close to becoming a
professional ballplayer as I would ever come.   I
continued to practice in the infield with the Yankees
throughout my two years at the Stadium, taking full
advantage of my good fortune.   Having sold Crosetti on
my capabilities, I believed that I had license to mix it up
with these great ballplayers.

Playing ball with the New York Yankees during
practice was the height of my experience with the club,
but just hanging around with the team in the clubhouse
was almost as much fun.   Big Pete Sheehy was such a

great guy and I truly appreciated how nice he was to me. Second in command to Big Pete Sheehy was Pete "Little Pete" Previte, who assisted Big Pete in the clubhouse. Little Pete was responsible for the clubhouse concession table and supplied all of the food, candy, soda and cigarettes for the team. Little Pete was a private guy who kept to himself and liked to smoke little gnarly, twisted black Di Nobili cigars that emitted a foul-smelling smoke. I was very familiar with these cigars because many of the older men in Little Italy would smoke them while playing cards outside of neighborhood cafes. The concession stand operated on an honor system, and to keep some type of record, Little Pete created a chart, displaying the names of all the players, with boxes drawn next to each name. The chart was hung on a wall near the stand and as each player took an item he would write it next to his name, and at the end of every home-stand, each player would settle up with Little Pete. On more than one occasion the supply of fresh fruit would become depleted so Little Pete sent me out to the Grand Concourse to buy a new supply. Even shopping for groceries in the Bronx for the Yankees was a thrilling experience for me.

In 1963 and 1964, for the away-games, Yankee ballplayers were given a food-allowance of $8.00 per day for concession items but had to pay their own expenses for the home games. Today in all of the home games, the teams are treated to gourmet meals and can eat and drink as much as they want for free, and, I suspect, for away-games are given substantial allowances to spend while travelling. In the 1960s the average ballplayer did not make a lot of money and many players had second jobs or other means of income. Some players sold cars or clothing in the off-season and some had other interests; Jim Bouton sold costume-jewelry for his wife's company; Yogi Berra and Phil Rizzuto owned a successful bowling alley in Clifton, New Jersey called *Rizzuto-Berra Lanes*. This just boggles my mind; to think that the star ballplayers today are paid more to play one game than the players in the 1960s earned for the entire season. For example, a star-quality pitcher today can earn $15 million per season. Based on playing 30 games per season, at that rate he's getting about *$5,000 per pitch!* Shortly before his very untimely passing in 1995, at the age of 63, Mickey Mantle was asked about the huge salaries of the day. "So Mickey, if you were in your prime today and the owner of the Yankees asked what you'd want, to play for the team, what would you tell him?" asked a reporter. Mickey just smiled that great smile and answered "Hello partner!"

When school was out during the summer of 1963 I was treated to my first airline flight, as the Yankees went on the road for a three-city, ten-game series; to Boston, Chicago and Baltimore. The trips always began with a bus ride to the airport, then onto the plane and then another bus ride to a hotel near the ballpark. These experiences were priceless, and travelling with professional ballplayers was not unlike travelling with my best friends on a school trip. On my first trip to

Chicago in August of 1963, my experiences reached a different, more man-of-the-world level. The bus pulled into the hotel and after the team exited and all of the baggage was distributed, I checked into my own room. The next night after unpacking my bag I headed down to the lobby and decided to take a short walk; to check out what was happening in the neighborhood. Walking toward the bus depot near the hotel in search of a magazine or newspaper, I noticed a very pretty young lady pacing back and forth. I headed in her direction and casually started a conversation. She had been waiting for friends for quite some time and was becoming worried that they had missed their connection. She was very good-looking and was only a few years older than myself, but I had to check in with the team, so I wished her luck. Before heading back to the hotel I stopped at a newsstand for a magazine, but the young lady was still on my mind, so after buying the magazine, and being a person who always worried about young ladies in distress, I decided to go back to see if she was still there. As I approached the depot I saw her, still pacing but with a very worried look on her face. "Where are you friends?" I asked. "I don't know and there is no way for me to contact them." the lovely, worried young lady said. "What are you going to do?" I asked. "I, I don't know. I just don't know." she said, her voice shaking and bordering on tears. "Listen. I'm with the New York Yankees" I said "and I'm staying at the hotel down the street. You are more than welcome to hang around with me in my hotel room until you decide what you want to do." When I look back on that experience I can't help but think that, years later, it may have inspired the Four Seasons' song *Oh What a Night.*

For the first time in my brief career with the New York Yankees, the next morning I was late for my duties as batboy. Having missed the mandatory 10:30 bus to Comiskey Park, I had to get to the ballpark by taxicab. When I arrived at the ballpark no one knew who I was and I almost panicked, until I remembered the Yankee ID Card in my wallet. When I got to the clubhouse Bruce Henry, the Yankee Travelling Secretary was steaming and was in no mood for any bullshit as he interrogated me, looking for answers. Bruce Henry was responsible for me and was about to send for the police when I did not respond to the banging on my hotel room door. He might even have been fired over such an event. Telling the truth to Mr. Henry, I was let off the hook but Frank Crosetti, in earshot of the discussion let the word out about the saucy dialogue. News of my "imagined" rendezvous travelled quickly through the clubhouse and continued into dinner that evening. I took a lot of abuse from everyone, because no one except Phil Linz and Joe Pepitone believed my excuse for being late. It should be understood by this point in my story that I was truly a most fortunate young man, for as the ribbing continued at the dinner table, situated near the front window of the hotel, that same very pretty young distressed damsel from the bus depot just happened to pass by that window, looked in and saw me. She came into the restaurant, walked over to the Yankee-filled table to tell me how very grateful she was for my kindness and my company the night before. She also apologized for leaving the hotel room before I had gotten up and for not having a chance to say goodbye. She had connected with her friends that afternoon and was hoping to see me before she left. When she kissed me goodbye and walked away from the table I didn't say one word; I just sat there grinning from ear to ear, and the Yankees also said nothing as they just stared at me, mouths wide open; heads shaking in wondrous disbelief. Her showing up that morning made the night before that much more satisfying and memorable.

By the time the team pulled into Baltimore I had been away from home for more than a week. I was having the time of my life, having travelled through three states and to three big cities; Boston, Chicago and Baltimore. When the team checked into the hotel in Baltimore I learned that I would be rooming with Tony Kubek. Tony was a great guy and we hit it off pretty well right from the beginning of the season. Born in Milwaukee, Wisconsin, Kubek joined the Yankees in 1957 and in a relatively short time, became one of the best infielders on the team. He had a wonderful outlook on life and was a genuinely nice guy. Though I never actually said anything to Tony about being homesick – to this day I don't know where Kubek ever got the idea that I was homesick – Kubek suspected that I missed my parents and that I just could not wait to see them, so, without my knowledge, Tony made special arrangements for my mother and father to come to Baltimore, have dinner, stay overnight and attend the game against the Orioles. As they arrived in town and were parking their car near the ballpark, a smart-ass parking attendant told them that they had wasted their time and money by travelling so far to watch the Yankees lose. Before my father could respond to the guy my mother assured the attendant that he was sadly misinformed by his bookmaker and that, hopefully, he had not wagered any of his tips on the game. New York defeated Baltimore soundly that day. Before they arrived I silently wished that Tony had not gone ahead and set this up, but after my mother and father left to go back to New York, I felt pretty good about seeing my parents and never forgot the very sweet act of kindness arranged by my good friend Tony Kubek. While this part of my story was being written in late 2013, I was called by cell-phone to confirm to which city Tony Kubek had invited my parents. I wasn't sure, but I knew who would know. "Hold on" I said. "I'll call my mother on the house line and ask her!" Within a moment my, then, 91 year old mother came to the phone. "Hey Ma, it's me, Anthony. Remember when you and daddy came to the away-game to watch me when I was a bat boy for the Yankees?" "Yes, of course I remember." she said. "What city was it Ma?" I asked. Without a moment's hesitation she said "It was Baltimore!" "Thanks Ma! I'll call you tomorrow." Sharp as a tack, my mother recalled the trip to Baltimore with my father in 1963.

The Yankees were having another good year in 1963 and I was enjoying my time with the team, in the clubhouse and on the field. My relationship with the players had, in a short time, become very warm and friendly and I came to respect and admire them in a number of ways. Three of the players, Phil Linz, Al Downing and Joe Pepitone, were only a few years older than me and I was able to relate to them in a more personal way. Phil Linz was from Baltimore, Maryland and had joined the Yankees in 1962. Not a New Yorker but he did have a New York attitude which I found extremely comforting. Phil was a good ballplayer and was the *super sub* for every infield position, and we became very good friends. He was a pretty funny guy and did everything he could to get a laugh out of me. For example, he did this crazy thing with his spit. He could make it bubble up and blow spit bubbles into the air. As dumb as it was, I couldn't ever do it myself; and I still can't. Another player, Al Downing, a good left handed pitcher, was only five years older than me. Years later, on April 8, 1974, Downing would become famous for giving up the pitch to Hank Aaron that turned into Aaron's record-breaking 715th home run, but I remember Al Downing for another reason. For such a young man, Downing seemed to sleep a lot; both in the clubhouse and in the dugout. He would be talking one minute and would nod off in the next; just conking out.

Suffering from chronic fatigue, Al Downing was most likely a victim of narcolepsy, commonly known as sleeping sickness. Another player was six years older and kind of adopted me as a kid-brother. Also a native New Yorker, he came from

Brooklyn and we became friends immediately; both of us really liking baseball and girls. Like me, he was always trying to get attention from the fans; especially the girl fans. One day I told him about my going on a date and he asked if I could hook him up with a friend of my date. This was easily accomplished and that night he picked me up in his car, and then we picked up our dates. After a quick dinner we drove around and then he found a quiet spot; for us to get to know each other. At some point he and his date left the car for a walk; a long walk. I would say that they really got to know each other as they returned to the car smiling, walking arm in arm. We dropped the girls off at a subway station and then he drove me home. It was pretty late and my father was not happy about it; nor was he too thrilled or impressed to hear my excuses for the late hour. I thought I'd be off the hook because I was driven home by a famous ballplayer, but my father was so pissed off that I was so late that he could not have cared less if it were Babe Ruth who was the culprit!

I hit it off pretty good as friends with a number of the players. One player in particular, Joe Pepitone, was a really good sport. He was, I believe, the first New York Yankee to use a hair dryer in the clubhouse, and he took a lot of ribbing on his constant use of the thing. That notoriety extended outside of the clubhouse and brought him the honor of having a hair salon named after him on Flatbush Avenue in Brooklyn. After all, Joe was a Brooklyn boy, famous in his youth for hitting a *Spaldeen* more than three sewers. I know Joe would have been an even better ballplayer if he had only dedicated himself more to the game. He had talent and was a natural and might have been one of the truly great players of all time.

One player who liked me a lot also liked to tease me a lot. As a third baseman Clete Boyer was just incredible; trapping, snagging and bare-handing anything that came anywhere near him. He also had a great throwing arm and could nail guys going to first while throwing from some very unusual positions. Boyer was from Cassville, Missouri, and was one of fourteen children. He joined the Yankees in 1957 but didn't get the chance to play third base until 1959. Clete's brother Ken played for the St. Louis Cardinals and in 1964, both men would become the first brothers in baseball history to hit home runs on opposing teams during a World Series.

I was a very respectful kid to all the players and could also spar with them when necessary. A running gag between us had Clete Boyer threatening me with the prospect of Boyer bringing his seventeen year old brother to the clubhouse, to beat me up if I got out of line, to which I would always say "Yea, yea. I'm really scared." One afternoon before the game the teasing took a different turn. "Hey Tony!" shouted Boyer in front of several players. "You know what? I think I really am going to bring my little brother in tomorrow to beat the crap out of you!" Feeling somewhat embarrassed by the comment made in front of so many players, I had had enough of the teasing. "I tell you what." I said. "Why don't you bring your little seventeen year old brother around, because when you do I'm going to crack both of you across the head with your own bat!" The team exploded into laughter and so did Boyer, realizing that he had pushed me too far. Of course my comment was not really made in anger because, recognizing that he was a pretty powerful guy, I knew that Boyer could twist me into a pretzel if he wanted to.

After the incident in the clubhouse Clete Boyer became a lot nicer to me and we hit it off pretty well, often having a catch before the game. As great a fielder as Boyer was, he was not a great hitter, often falling into slumps. Though the Yankees could carry a 220 hitter, Clete was not happy about his own batting performances. One afternoon while approaching the on-deck circle, Boyer called to me. "Hey Tony! Bring me something that will get me a hit." Not skipping a beat I reached for Elston Howard's bat; one of the largest in the line-up. Clete Boyer looked at me while hefting the weight of the bat. "You might get a piece of the ball with this thing." I advised, as Boyer headed for the plate. It was just another one of the great memories that I have since cherished, because Clete Boyer got more than a piece of the ball that afternoon, he got the whole thing and crashed it into the stands for a home run. After rounding the bases, Boyer ran over to me and shook my hand. I was a hero. In his next at-bat, using the same bat, Boyer struck out magnificently and went back to using his own bat.

The 1963 Yankees had an excellent pitching staff and Jim Bouton was one of its stars. Jim was from Newark, New Jersey and started his major league career in 1962 when he joined the Yankees. Bouton had a number of great pitches, including an excellent and violent overhand curveball, that would cause his hat to

Hal Reniff & Clete Boyer

fly off after almost every pitch, but on one afternoon at the Stadium none of his pitches worked. After giving up several runs in the top of the first inning, Bouton was pulled off the mound. Storming off the field he headed for the showers. As he walked into the clubhouse Frank Crosetti and I were hanging out while the Yankees were on the field and we watched as Bouton began ripping off his shirt; expletives flying along with his buttons. Turning to me and whispering, Frank Crosetti said "If he was that tough he'd still be on the mound, pitching!" Steve Hamilton was a good left handed pitcher as well and at 6' 7" I considered him to be a gentle giant. Hamilton had a great slow pitch he called the *Folly Floater*; an exaggerated change-up that he threw fifteen feet in the air, in a high arc that seemed to float over home plate. Bill Stafford was an equally nice guy to me and one of the star pitchers on the team. The pitchers would practice on a mound that was behind home plate and one afternoon I asked Stafford to teach me how to throw a slider. The slider was a tough pitch to hit; a quick-breaking shorter curveball. Handing me the ball and showing me the proper way to grip it, Stafford told me to give it a try. I threw a perfect pitch, six inches over the right corner of home plate, and Stafford just stared in amazement. "Okay kid" said Stafford "It's your turn to teach me how to throw that pitch!" I never threw one that good in my life. The Yankee pitching staff recognized my capabilities as a pitcher, well maybe my lack of capabilities, and they were more than happy to help me improve those talents. As I always used to say, you can't make a steak sandwich out of hot dogs!

I was not hard to like and every Yankee treated me as one of their own. I befriended each player in an open and genuine manner and spoke with them like older brothers. There probably wasn't a nicer player on the team than Bobby Richardson; a gentle gentleman to me and to every other guy in the clubhouse. Bobby was a soft spoken guy from Sumpter, South Carolina, who was as nice in person as he was written about in the press. He played for the Yankees from 1955 through the 1966 season and had just come off the best year of his career in 1962. I don't remember ever hearing him swear or seeing him lose his temper. He was definitely one of the best defensive players in the game and played a major role for the Yankees in his day.

Richardson thought that I was a character and would marvel at my demeanor and New York attitude. He did more than marvel I think, because looking at this skinny sixteen year old character who smoked, chewed tobacco and constantly joked around, I believe he also prayed for me. In keeping with his love of the game, after retiring from professional baseball Richardson became coach at the University of South Carolina and later, as a born-again Christian, became the leader of the *Fellowship of Christian Athletes*. Elston Howard was another great ballplayer to have met in those years, and as big and gentle as he was, it was good to know that he was also a great player. Elston Howard was born in St. Louis, Missouri in 1929 and was a recognized athlete by the time he got to high school. In 1948 he was offered scholarships from a number of universities but turned them down; opting to play with the Negro leagues instead. He signed with the Yankees in 1950, spent four years in the minors, and in 1955 became the first African-American to play major league baseball for the Yankees. Elston Howard was a great catcher but it was hard for the Yankees to keep him behind home plate with the likes of Yogi Berra around, so he was moved around to the outfield and to first base, to keep him in the lineup. When catching for Whitey Ford, Howard had this little trick of secretly scoring the ball on one of his shin guards; creating a small cut and enabling Whitey to throw some fancy pitches; some that travelled like *spitballs* because of how Howard's little cuts in the ball would alter its flight. Today, with all of the cameras filming players from all different angles, it would be very difficult to hide such trickery. In those days even the groundskeepers would get into the act, giving advantages to the home team. For example, when they cut the grass along the third and first base foul lines, they would leave the grass slightly higher at the edge, enabling bunts to stay longer in fair territory. I think this happened in every stadium and ballpark, so I guess it all evened out in the end. One day, Elston showed up late for practice, explaining that he had had a minor but painful accident. Turns out that he had closed his zipper too fast, before all of the body parts had been returned to their designated places. No one looked him in the eye or joked about the mishap until he, himself laughed out loud and invited a few harsh but very funny comments from his teammates.

Whitey Ford did okay, regardless of who was catching; holding on to one of the best winning percentages for many years. Whitey Ford, a Yankee legend, was born in Astoria, Queens in the heart of New York City in 1928. He signed with the Yankees in 1947 and never left; except for a stint with the US Army in 1951 and 1952 during the Korean War. The name Whitey, came from Ford's very light blond hair. Whitey had a personal relief pitcher, Luis Arroyo, who came into a game whenever necessary. Arroyo relieved pitchers in more than 160 games and personally saved 21 games for Ford. The two players became even more famous when they reenacted their friendship for a *Lifesavers* TV commercial.

In addition to my regular responsibilities, Frank Crosetti also relied on me as more than just batboy. At the start of a game the Yankees were responsible for supplying six dozen new baseballs; to be given to the home plate umpire throughout the game as needed. Before each game all of the umpires would get together to rub a little damp *Mississippi Mud* on the new baseballs to reduce the sheen, enabling the batters to better see each pitch. Mississippi Mud was, in fact, mud that actually came from Mississippi and was stored in small, covered cans. Throughout the game, as balls were fouled off, the home plate umpire would signal to the home team for additional balls. I was charged with the additional responsibility of inventory control; in charge of the sack that held all of the balls, keeping tabs on the number of balls remaining, and if the level fell below one dozen balls I would inform Crosetti who would signal for more from the clubhouse. The home plate umpire would also determine if a ball needed to be removed from play and would often take a ball out of the game, to be discarded. However, if I determined that a ball was not so bad, I would put it back into the umpire's bag, because in addition to managing the inventory, Greg Cahoon and I had to rub mud on the balls as well, and I hated having to do it. By recycling balls that were, in my unsolicited opinion, still acceptable for use, I would make them last as long as possible and would also make fewer trips to the clubhouse. Whenever the Yankees were on the field, I would be certain to give the umpire the worst balls in the bag, making it that much more difficult for the opposing team to hit and helping to give my beloved Yankees an edge. Again, in those days there was none of this tossing foul balls to fans; seen in every game played today. Back then, I think Crossetti would have shot me if I threw a ball into the stands. I wanted to, but it just never happened.

I had a number of memorable experiences during the 1963 season; getting to know the players so well, practicing with them on the field, receiving tips on how to pitch from some of the best players in the major leagues, and being in Yankee Stadium with thousands of cheering and loving fans. My luck continued when the Yankees won the Pennant and I could look forward to attending another World Series in Yankee Stadium as well as in California; against the Los Angeles Dodgers. Once again the baseball event of the year would have New York buzzing; another former New York team – from Brooklyn – playing against the incumbent World Champion and current New York team from the Bronx. The Yankees had a good pitching staff led by Whitey Ford, Bill Stafford and Stan Williams, and home run sluggers like Mantle and Maris; the word *sweep* was in the air. Los Angeles had an excellent pitching squad as well; Don Drysdale, Johnny Podres and Sandy Koufax.

On October 2, 1963 I would get a chance, in person, to witness some of the very best pitching I would ever see in my life. Sandy Koufax was a native New Yorker by way of Boro Park, Brooklyn, who once had aspirations of becoming a professional basketball player; most of the batters who faced him wished he had chosen basketball. During the three years that I spent at Yankee Stadium, and in all the years since, I have never seen or known another professional baseball pitcher who even approached throwing a baseball the way that Sandy Koufax could. In Game One of the series Koufax would be pitching against Whitey Ford, whose own reputation preceded him. Once again I would be present at a record-setting World Series game as Koufax struck out 15 batters, shattering the 14-batter record held previously by Carl Erskine, and he would hold that record for five years until Bob Gibson struck out 17 batters in 1968. I had never seen such a talented, focused pitcher as Koufax and was absolutely blown away by this legend of professional baseball as the

Dodgers took game one 5-2. Game Two of the 1963 series would see the Yankees lose again to the Dodgers 4-1. One other thing for which Sandy Koufax was recognized was his loyalty to his Jewish faith; never playing on the Sabbath. It never happened during my experience with the Yankees, but I sure did wish that during the 1963 Series, at least one of the games would be scheduled on the Sabbath.

I was invited to travel to California to attend the World Series games against the Dodgers, and although the Yankees were down two games, I had great faith in my heroes and was very excited about the long flight to Los Angeles. It was during that long flight to the west coast that I observed an unforgettable sight. The gentle giant Steve Hamilton was absolutely terrified about flying and this endless flight to California was really bugging the hell out of him. There he sat, all 6' 7" of him, clutching a set of rosary beads in his huge hands, praying to The Good Lord for the plane to land safely and soon. No one ever bothered Steve Hamilton about this.

In Game Three the Yankees would face ace right-hander Don Drysdale, who would shutout the Bronx Bombers and give up only four hits. That evening after the game the Yankees were in a pretty foul mood and each player seemed to wander off into his own space. In the hotel, sitting by himself and muttering, Phil Linz was busy writing numbers on a piece of paper. I walked over to him and asked what the heck he was doing. "I'm calculating the loser's share of the World Series." said the multi-talented super substitute. "What the hell are you talking about Phil" I exclaimed. "There are still four more games to play!" "You saw how we fared against Drysdale today, didn't you kid?" Linz posed. "Yea. Sure. Of course I did!" I said. "Do you know who's pitching for the Dodgers tomorrow?" Linz asked. "Of course I do." I said. "Do you think I've been sleeping? Koufax is pitching tomorrow!" I told Phil. He then laid out his reason for all of the calculating and mumbling "Well Tony, you see, based on our performance against Koufax in Game One and on our performance against Drysdale today in Game Three; based on the odds of our beating Koufax tomorrow, I've been trying to calculate the losers' share of the World Series receipts!" I just stared at Phil Linz and then exploded into a fit of laughter. Of course Phil Linz' odds-making talent was keen and on the money, as the Los Angeles Dodgers, led by the incomparable Sandy Koufax, defeated the New York Yankees in Game Four by a score of 2-1, sweeping the Yankees in four straight games. Linz agreed, as did most players and fans, that there was no one who dominated the game like Sandy Koufax; probably the very best pitcher who ever lived. In the final game of that series however, I would have another memorable moment as Mantle, facing the incomparable Sandy Koufax, crushed the hardest ball that I had ever seen my idol hit, and homered off the ace pitcher. I don't think that ball rose over twelve feet, as it soared across the field. I swear I saw smoke trailing behind it as it blasted into the stands. The same day, the long flight back to New York seemed just as long for all of the other New York Yankees as it did for poor Steve Hamilton.

1963 Yankees - Tony on bottom right

Jim Bouton & Ralph Terry

Elston Howard

Tony Kubek

Roger Maris

Mike Hegan & Jim Hegan

Pedro González & Bobby Richardson

Steve Hamilton & Héctor López

Al Downing & Mel Stottlemyre

Bill Stafford & Johnny Blanchard

Jim Gleeson & Frankie Crosetti

Tony being interviewed before World Series game

New York Yankees

OFFICE MEMORANDUM DATE October 21, 1963

To   Tony-

Here's the list you wanted - just be sure you use it
for just yourself - don't give the address to any of your
friends.

Office Memorandum

1963

PLAYERS' WINTER ADDRESSES

		CODE
HOUK	...le River, N.J.	201 DA 7
BERRA	...d, Montclair, N.J.	201 PI 6
CROSETTI	...ve., Stockton, Cal.	209 HO 3
HEGAN	..., Lakewood 7, Ohio	216 AC 6
LONG	North Adams, Mass.	413 MO 3
MURRAY	...ve., Oakland, N.J.	201 337
SAIN	..., Walnut Ridge, Arkansas	
SEGER	...d, Richmond 28, Va.	703 CO 6
SOARES	..., San Diego 6, Cal.	714 AC 4
HENRY	...ve., Westfield, N.J.	201 AD 3
BLANCHARD	..., No., Golden Valley 22, Minn	612 JA 6
BOUTON	...e, Ridgewood, N.J.	201 OL 2
BOYER	..., River Edge, N.J.	201 489
BRIDGES	...Avenue, Jackson, Miss.	601 366
BRIGHT	...a, Sacramento, Cal.	
DALEY	...ace, Orange, Cal.	714 63
DOWNING	...us, Trenton, N.J.	609 OW 5
FORD	...une, Lake Success, N.Y.	516 HU 2
GIBBS	..., Grenada, Miss.	601 1979
GONZALEZ	...Pedro de Macoris, Dominican Rep.	
HAMILTON	..., Morehead, Kentucky	
HOWARD	...te, Teaneck, N.J.	201 TE
KUBEK	...t, Nassau, Wisconsin	715 VI
KUNKEL	...ue, Paterson, N.J.	201 270
LINZ	..., Baltimore 24, Maryland	301 BR
LOPEZ	...West Hempstead, L.I., N.Y.	516 RO
MANTLE	...e, Dallas 25, Texas	214 EM
MARIS	...il, Independence, Mo.	816 CL
METCALF	...e, Wisconsin Rapids, Wisconsin	715 HA
PEPITONE	..., Bronx, N.Y.	TA
RERD	...	601 50
RENIFF	..., Ontario, Cal.	714 YJ
RICHARDSON	...Sumter, South Carolina	803 77
STAFFORD	...Yonkers, N.Y.	
TERRY	...d, Kansas	316 AT
TRESH	...t. Pleasant, Michigan	77
WILLIAMS	..., Lakewood, Cal.	213 429

Players' winter addresses

83

Fantasy

Reality

Phil Rizzuto

Whitey Ford

Spring 1964

In November of 1963 I turned seventeen and was convinced, once again, that having spent the last two years at Yankee Stadium and having had the great fortune of working, practicing and travelling with the New York Yankees, my life was complete and the world was a wonderful place. At the end of the 1963 season, before the World Series, I was told that I would be invited back to the stadium in the spring of 1964, to be the official New York Yankee Batboy for the team, so my birthday present had come a little early and my good luck continued for another year. But at the tender age of seventeen I would also soon learn that the world was not so wonderful after all and that, in a flash, a young man could awaken from a beautiful dream and be thrown into a nightmare.

Fewer than three weeks after my seventeenth birthday, on November 22, 1963, in the blink of an eye, John F. Kennedy, the most popular American President of the twentieth century was cut down by an assassin's bullet and the world as I had known it came crashing down. The country wept and mourned and demanded answers, but as had occurred after the Cuban Missile Crisis, the nation would not know for decades, the truth about who killed this beloved man, why he was killed and how his murder could have been so perfectly and so diabolically covered up. What stays with me about those terrible days is my watching the live television broadcast of Jack Ruby shooting Lee Harvey Oswald in the stomach as he was being transferred from the Dallas police station. I remember people dancing in the streets because the assumed killer of President Kennedy had himself been killed. Like millions of other viewers, I had no idea how unfortunate Oswald's death was to the already hapless investigation of the assassination. Political turmoil and assassination plots are rather complicated topics to comprehend, even for political scientists and history professors, but for a seventeen year old kid whose entire life, so far, had been devoted to baseball, it was impossible to comprehend. The only thing that I could do at the time was to try to remember how fine a man President Kennedy was - his great smile, the New England accent - and to try to concentrate on more positive thoughts.

The coming 1964 baseball season would find Big Pete and Little Pete still running the Yankee clubhouse, and Frank Crosetti would still serve as Yankee coach, a position he would hold through the 1968 season, but the management had turned around a bit. Ralph Houk would become General Manager for the team and Yogi Berra would become Yankee Manager. Houk was a player's manager and had a quick temper; often flying onto the field to argue with an umpire when a call had not gone well for the Yankees. Ralph Houk was a pretty big guy and a Marine. All the players respected him and no one would dare to mess with him.

Most New York Yankee fans believed that Yogi Berra had contributed so much to the team and that he was as important to the Yankee dynasty as Mickey Mantle, Roger Maris and Whitey Ford. Lawrence Peter Berra, a first generation American, was born in St. Louis, Missouri in 1925 and was one of five children born to Pietro and Paolina Berra. The nickname *Yogi* is attributed to his resemblance to a Hindu yogi, whenever he would sit with his arms and legs crossed, waiting to bat during minor league games. Another famous ballplayer, Joe Garagiola, was a schoolmate and childhood friend of Yogi's in St. Louis. Yogi actually lost out to Garagiola in 1942 when both friends tried out for the St. Louis Cardinals. Yogi served his country in *World War II* in the *US Navy* as a gunner's mate during the *D-Day Invasion*. He had been playing baseball since he was a kid, was quite good and developed many of his skills in local minor leagues; including the Newark Bears. Yogi signed with the Yankees in 1946 and was outstanding in his day. From 1949 through 1955 Yogi led the team in RBIs. Meeting this Yankee legend and having the chance to work with him in the dugout just added to my great experiences as a batboy.

Yogi was one of the greatest catchers in professional baseball and a fair Yankee manager. In my opinion, what worked against Yogi was that he was well-liked by all the players and became more of a friend than a manager. The 1964 season would present him with a number of challenges; both on and off the field. As I looked forward to my third opening day at Yankee Stadium the same excitement that I felt in 1962 was still evident as April 16th drew closer. I would be back again, hanging around with my heroes, and though I had spent so much time with the team the year before, I would never be completely relaxed in their presence. The team now referred to me as Tony and as the season began a few of the players wanted to know what I had been up to since the end of last year's season. A few of the players also talked about the Kennedy assassination and about how terribly upset they had been for months after; most were just anxious to start playing ball.

All of the players had become very comfortable with me as batboy and often included me in their pranks; sometimes I was party to a prank and sometimes I was the target. One afternoon during batting practice in Comiskey Park the team decided to test my sense of humor. It had been raining that morning so the drums for the tarpaulins were rolled onto the field and several empty tarp-drums had been rolled out into the outfield. In those days the drums were kept on the field; not removed and stored the way the teams do today. As balls were flying onto the field a number of them found their way onto the open ends of the tarp-drum in centerfield. I had been shagging balls with the team so Frank Crosetti asked me to get the balls in the drum. "Hey Tony" shouted Crow. "Reach into the drum and get those balls." Without hesitation I ran over to the drum and grabbed a few balls that were lying near the rim, inside, and threw them back to the mound. "C'mon Tony" chided Crosetti. "Go inside the damn thing and get all of them. There's got to be dozens in there!" Again I ran to the drum and stooped down to look into the twenty-foot long, three foot high cylinder, but I did not just run in this time. "I'm not going in there. It's filthy!" I shouted. "I'll ruin my uniform!" This invited a more assertive command from Crosetti. I stooped down and stepped in. "Go in further!" shouted the third base coach. "There are a lot more balls in the center." I couldn't understand why Crosetti was so insistent about my going into the cylinder drum; why he was so uncharacteristically demanding. I did, however, accept that his paranoia was well-founded. In those years, baseballs were always salvaged; never, for example tossed to fans the way they are today. Every baseball would need to be retrieved and it was the batboy's job to get them. But something seemed fishy about this as I looked around and did not see any of the Yankees near the damned thing. Of course the whole thing was a set-up and as soon as I stepped in closer to the center of the filthy, dark and dank drum, Yankees appeared from out of thin air and began to roll the drum all around the field; in front of 35,000 screaming, laughing fans. Some of the finest expletives that had ever been invoked in my native Little Italy began to echo inside the drum and pour out, directed at as many New York Yankees as I could hear as I tumbled inside. Satisfied that they had tortured me enough, the drum was rolled back to centerfield and I emerged from the ride from hell. Covered from head to toe in grease, grime and other unidentifiable filth, I was steaming mad and let everyone know it. I did laugh to myself because my street-smarts told me not to go into the drum, but my sense of obligation got the better of me and I fell for the gag; I was really ticked-off and did not have another uniform and would have to sit this game out.

Back in the neighborhood my position as New York Yankee Batboy was now, very well-known and I was often the topic of conversation among my friends and neighbors. One afternoon Joe DiMaggio stopped in for espresso at Café Roma, right across the street from my apartment. Someone in the cafe mentioned to DiMaggio that a local kid was a New York Yankee batboy and another person told one of the kids hanging outside to "Go find Anthony!" The neighborhood was scoured until I could be found. A number of my friends followed me into the café as I proudly introduced himself to the famous *Yankee Clipper* and told him that we were kind of related in a way; both part of the greatest team in history. What a thrill to meet my father's hero and one of the greatest ballplayers of all time. He was very nice to me and seemed genuinely interested in my batboy experiences, asking how I got the position and what I thought of the team today. Again, speaking so casually with such a famous ballplayer about the Yankees, in front of my friends and neighbors, really made me feel incredibly lucky and so very special.

Having been seen on television, I was starting to feel like somebody; resulting in envy by some and admiration by others. A number of my neighborhood friends attended *Transfiguration Catholic School* in Chinatown, a small well respected school in Little Italy, and one day a few friends came to me to ask a favor. Sister Paul Michel was one of the instructors at the school and in addition to doing the Lord's work she also loved baseball; a native Michiganite, she particularly loved the Detroit Tigers. The guys told Sister Paul about my being a batboy for the Yankees and all about my experiences and escapades at Yankee Stadium; how I told them so many great stories about hanging around with famous ballplayers from all over the country. They promised her that they would ask me to try to get some Tiger autographs when the team came to the Stadium to face the Yankees. She was amused by the stories and by their kind offer but did not think much about it. I promised my friends that I would try; assuring them that it wouldn't be a problem for someone so close to the action. I also met with Sister Paul a number of times and asked her about her love of the team. She was a true Tigers fan and enjoyed sharing her knowledge of the game. In early May of the 1964 season the Tigers came to town, losing a heartbreaker by one run. Before that game I walked over to the visitors' dugout and asked the batboy to please get all the Tigers to sign a baseball for someone special. The team was happy to accommodate, all signed the ball and the visitor's batboy presented me with the trophy. The next day Sister Paul's students told her that someone was going to bring her a present and, again, she dismissed their comments as a prank. That afternoon I walked into the school like a visiting dignitary and presented the autographed ball to Sister Paul. She could not believe her eyes and that her students were on the level about the Yankee batboy and she was absolutely thrilled with the very meaningful treasure. She thanked me for my kindness and, cherishing this wonderful gift from such an avid young Yankee fan, Sister Paul later wrote to me to express her gratitude. That warm note from Sister Paul is one of my most prized possessions from my days as New York Yankee batboy.

As the season evolved, I wasn't sure if I would be attending another New York Yankee World Series in 1964. The team seemed to be struggling and the mood in the clubhouse was getting darker. Coming off a win in the last game of a three-game series in Baltimore, the team headed for Chicago with a sense of optimism, but that feeling would soon evaporate. The White Sox swept the four-game series, sending the Bronx Bombers on their way with their tails between their legs. There was silence in the visitors' clubhouse after the game and silence on the bus as the team left town, but the silence on the bus would soon be broken by the sound of a harmonica. Phil Linz was only a few years older than me, so the infielder and the batboy hit it off fairly well; talking about school and girls and baseball. Phil Linz was a very good infielder but he was not a very good harmonica player, and his attempt to entertain his fellow Yankee teammates was not having a great deal of success. As his amateurish playing continued and he jumped from tune to tune, a few of the players started to come out of the doldrums while a few others became annoyed. One of the more annoyed bus riders was Yogi Berra. Yogi was in a foul mood after the series against the White Sox and was neither entertained nor amused by Linz' poor talents. Sitting in the front of the bus and shouting to Linz, who was sitting in back, the Yankee Manager told the young musician to stop playing that "damned instrument." Unable to hear his manager, Linz continued to play. Yogi became hotter. "Hey Linz" shouted Yogi. "Stop that noise before I shove that thing where the sun don't shine!" This time Phil Linz heard something coming from the front of the bus and asked "What did he say?" Mickey Mantle, one of the great Yankee pranksters, was sitting across from him and told Linz "He said to play louder!" So the young infielder played as loud as he could and became more animated in his performance. Yogi had had it and bolted from his seat. Charging towards the back of the bus and screaming in an expletive-filled rage, Yogi leaned into Phil Linz and angrily said "Didn't I tell you to stop playing that thing!" With this Linz tossed the harmonica to Yogi and said "Here! Maybe you'd like to play it!" In mid-air Yogi swatted at the damned thing, propelling it across the aisle, crashing smartly into the knee of Joe Pepitone, who wailed unnecessarily, faking severe pain and anguish. I wanted to get under my seat, because I didn't know if I could hold back my laughter. The *harmonica story* has been told a million times and in a million ways, but I was lucky enough to actually be on the bus that day; to bear witness to a really funny and memorable event.

The harmonica incident did not go unnoticed, nor did it go unrecorded, as a few sports-writers accompanying the team on the bus jotted down a blow-by-blow description of the event. The story spread like wildfire, was on the front page of newspapers around the country, and at the very next game on the road against Baltimore, as the Yankees took the field, Oriole fans began throwing plastic harmonicas onto the field. I believed that the harmonica incident was just what the Yankees needed to get the team back on track, because instead of suffering humiliation from the affair, the team became driven and inspired, playing great baseball and going on to win the *1964 American League Pennant*. In addition to the harmonicas thrown onto the field in Baltimore, I believe that there was another bit of good luck that helped the team to win the Pennant that year. In early September I attended the famous *Feast of San Gennaro* in Little Italy, famous for its parade, great food, games and attractions. Skillfully playing one of the games at the Feast, I won a very cute plush-toy poodle and brought it to the clubhouse. I marked it *1964,*designating it as the Yankees' hopeful *Pennant mascot* and placed it on a table near the door inside of the clubhouse, insuring that every Yankee that passed it on the way out would see it and become inspired. When the team did indeed win the Pennant in 1964, I was given credit for the good luck charm and was photographed with the toy poodle and with Dan Topping Jr., the owner's son. I was also interviewed about the mascot by Yankee announcer and former Yankee ballplayer, Jerry Coleman.

Tony after Yankees clinched '64 pennant, being interviewed
by Jerry Coleman & Dan Topping Jr.

I felt very much like a part of the team and carried out my role as batboy as if I were as important to the Yankees as one of the team's players. I was a capable ballplayer, but I knew that my chances for advancing much further were non-existent. On another memorable occasion I did pretend to be a professional ballplayer as well as a highly sought after candidate by major league scouts. While in Chicago for an away-game series, I roomed with one of the Yankee relief pitchers, known for carrying on an active social life. As the Yankees travelled around the country, it was a common occurrence for the team to be greeted by hordes of young ladies – groupies of the day – whenever the Yankees came to town. One evening, knowing that my roommate would be otherwise occupied and would be away from our hotel, I met two young ladies in the lobby and invited them up to our room for a little entertainment. I was, in fact, under the legal drinking age but, having developed special skills while growing up in Little Italy, I managed to get a bottle of good wine to bring to our private party. We were having a good old time when there was a knock on the door. As I opened the door a very attractive woman stood in the doorway, stared a bit, came in and asked to see my roommate. After a little while, the two other young ladies decided to leave. I waved goodbye to them and proceeded to explain to the socialite that my roommate would not be returning that evening. Disappointed in not having seen her primary target she now wanted to know who I was and if I were part of the Yankee organization. Being an equally capable story teller I spun a very fine yarn about how the Yankees were trying to get me to sign a professional contract with the team because they, as well as a number of other teams, had been scouting me; how they were talking about a pretty hefty contract as well as a huge signing bonus. Having been tempted by offers from other major league teams, I lied, I was somewhat torn by my love for New York and the Yankees and the possibility of moving to California. The attractive young woman was a bit older than me, but she certainly wasn't any more insightful, and she fell for my yarn, hook, line and sinker. She also fell for me that evening, and, for the second time in my batboy career, I was almost late again for another game, the next day.

The sky was bright blue the next day and the stands were filled with cheering White Sox fans. Energized by my good fortune the night before, I was in a great mood that afternoon, addressing every batboy responsibility with great enthusiasm. As always, I loved the attention from the crowd and really looked forward to the fans that day as the very popular New York Yankee batboy. The crowd watched me having a catch with one of the players but one member of the crowd was not paying attention to my throwing or catching capabilities. Maybe my luck had changed or maybe it was running out, because sitting in the stands, very near the Yankee dugout, taking in all of my batboy routine, was the very same attractive young woman from the evening before. Shooting an icy stare into my widely opened eyes the socialite, realizing that she had not been with a soon to be professional ballplayer the night before, but with a common, story-telling, lying batboy, stood up and mouthed several well-formed expletives concerning deceitfulness and lies, viciously attacking my character; she then stormed out of her seat and left. A few of the Yankees were in earshot of her tirade and just stared at me; laughing and shaking their heads in amazement.

Returning to Yankee Stadium for the next series of games with the Red Sox, I was going about my activities in the clubhouse when Big Pete asked to speak with me for a minute. He told me that the Yankee ball-boy, Greg Cahoon, was going to be out the next day and that it was standard procedure to ask the batboy for the visiting team to fill in as ball boy. Immediately my wheels started turning and I asked Big Pete to consider a different plan. "Pete, would it be possible for me to ask my best friend in the neighborhood to be the ball-boy for the day?" "I don't know Tony" said Big Pete "That's not how it's done." I would not let this go and continued to plead with Big Pete. "But this is my best friend in Little Italy and it's only for one day and I swear that I'll be responsible for him. What do you say?" Once again my skills, good luck and persistence resulted in events going my way as Big Pete caved-in to the badgering, pleading and begging and agreed to accept my plan. "Wow!" I thought to myself. "I'm going to have a chance to make another New York City kid lucky." That afternoon I raced home to find Junior Gondolfo; to tell him of his good fortune. I was going to have a lot of fun telling him about this really amazing opportunity. I spotted him on

the street and called out to him. "Hey Junior" I called.
"I gotta talk to you. I need you to do me a favor; if you
can do it." I explained to him how the Yankees needed
a replacement ball-boy for the next day's game and how
I convinced the clubhouse manager to let me select the
lucky kid. Junior just stared at me. "Yea, right." Then
he looked at me a bit more carefully. "Are you shitting
me, Anthony?" asked Junior, knowing my odd and often
cruel sense of humor. "Because if you are; if this is just
more of the usual bullshit..." I swore to Junior that I
was on the level and that he should never doubt my
sincerity again. "You're not kidding?" Junior asked
again. "I'm not kidding." I patiently replied. A series
of "Holy shits!" followed my assurance to my good friend.
The next day we travelled together to the Stadium and
showed up at the security booth. "Who's this Tony?"
asked the guard. "He's with me." I explained confidently
and then escorted Junior through the underground
tunnels of Yankee Stadium. As I had done before,
Junior just stared at the walls and at the floor as we
walked through these famous corridors. I took him right
through the clubhouse, passing Mickey Mantle, Roger
Maris, Whitey Ford, Tony Kubek and a number of other
Yankees as we headed for the laundry room that was the
batboys' private domain. As soon as we stepped into
the doorway of the laundry room Junior grabbed me by
the lapels of my jacket and started shaking me violently.
"Did you see who that was? Do you know who we just
passed in there?" Like myself and so many other New
York kids, Junior Gondolfo was also a huge fan of
Mickey Mantle and Roger Maris and of all the New York

Yankees and he just went berserk when he realized how close he had just been to his idol and to his heroes. Seeing my friend in such an excited state after just one encounter with the team, I realized how truly lucky I was to have spent so much time at Yankee Stadium for the past three seasons, and by witnessing Junior's reaction, the appreciation of that experience finally sank in. I gave Junior an equally ill-fitting uniform to wear and the two of us went out onto the field to have a catch. I felt a sensation of immense satisfaction as I watched my friend's reactions to all of the activities on the field that day and I will never forget how much fun we had that afternoon, and Junior Gondolfo never forgot my thoughtfulness and generosity in sharing my own dream with such a good friend from the neighborhood. We have not seen each other in almost forty years but I'm certain that our friendship would start up from where it left off, if we were to run into each other today.

Another visitor to the Yankee clubhouse one afternoon may have left with a different recollection of the experience. One of the great television programs for young audiences in 1964 was *Wonderama*, hosted by an extremely lovable guy named Sonny Fox. The broadcasts were live in those days and Wonderama was a kind of reality show for its time, with Sonny Fox selecting members of the audience for various contests and games. One write-in contest was called *Batboy for a Day* and offered the lucky winner the prize of spending an entire day at Yankee Stadium with the New York Yankees; the winner that Saturday morning was a very happy nine year old kid. A few days later the Yankee front office delivered the lucky winner to the dugout and placed me and Greg Cahoon in charge of the kid who, at nine years of age, turned out to be extremely difficult to control. Running back and forth in the dugout, asking a million questions; touching everything in the dugout – the kid was a disaster. I called him *Kidzilla*. The last straw may have been the kid's comment after one of the Yankees had struck out. In earshot of Yogi Berra the kid said "Why did he swing at that pitch?" Yogi was not happy about the kid being there in the first place and signaled to me. "Tony, please do something with this kid before I ......" growled the Yankee manager. I did not let Yogi finish his sentence and told him "I'll take care of it!" Now, Yogi Berra had three sons of his own and was not totally unfamiliar with how young boys can behave, but this kid was something else. Taking the excitable youngster by the hand, I told him that when the Yankees go onto the field the batboys always go into the clubhouse to watch the game on television, so I was going to show him what they do in the clubhouse. Within about five minutes the kid became bored with the tour of the clubhouse so I took him to the snack table and gave him a nice selection of candy and soda, and then he sat him down to watch TV. This kid did not need a sugar-rush to make him any more jumpy or any more excitable, and he was out of his chair in a flash, demanding to go back to the dugout and onto the field. "But this is what real batboys do during a game!" I lied unconvincingly. The kid would have none of that, so back to the dugout we went. Fortunately the Yankees were now ahead, as Yogi looked at my face and let out a big laugh. "Just keep him out of my hair and try to tire him out or something." said Yogi. Greg and I did our best and the kid finally settled down on the bench, chatting up players and rooting for the home team. When I think about that kid today I would have to say that he suffered from A.D.D. He was non-stop and would not or could not focus on anything.

The 1964 season did end well for the Yankees, though they won the Pennant by only one game over the Chicago White Sox; I would be treated to another World Series, this time against the St. Louis Cardinals. I would attend every game of the 1964 World Series and would see Mickey Mantle hit two home runs in the series, Maris hit one and Joe Pepitone hit a Grand Slam in Game Six, but I would not see my beloved Yankees win the series as the Cardinals defeated the Bombers in Game Seven. It would've been great to have seen the team win the last game in my last year as New York Yankee batboy – something I would not learn until the following year · but for three years I was still part of baseball history, if only a small part, and my heart would remain forever warmed, forever touched by the incredible experience of a lifetime.

1964 James Monroe
High School Yearbook
And
New York Yankee Autographs

When I graduated from James Monroe High School in 1964 I received my copy the school's yearbook and couldn't wait to bring it to Yankee Stadium so that all the Yankee ballplayers could autograph it for me.

The following pages show a number of autographs in the yearbook from my pals on the team. Some are funny, some are warm and a few are sarcastic, but each and every autograph brings back great memories of my incredible years at Yankee Stadium with the great New York Yankees.

To Tony
- The biggest hot-dog
Bat-boy we have
had since I've been
with the Yankees.
Your Pal
Mickey Mantle

MONROVIAN
PUBLISHED BY THE SENIOR CLASS
JAMES MONROE HIGH SCHOOL
BRONX, NEW YORK JUNE 1964

3

To Tony,
Best of Huck,
HD Downing

FOREIGN LANGUAGE DEPARTMEN
Mrs. Dreyfus; Mr Masella; Mrs. Ber

To Tony
Congratulations
on
Graduation
Buddy Russid

ART AND PHOTOGRAPHY STAFF: *Seated, Left to Right—*Aida
Fields; Marie Soldano; *Typist,* Caroline Crawford; *Standing—*
John McWilliams; Barry Feldman.

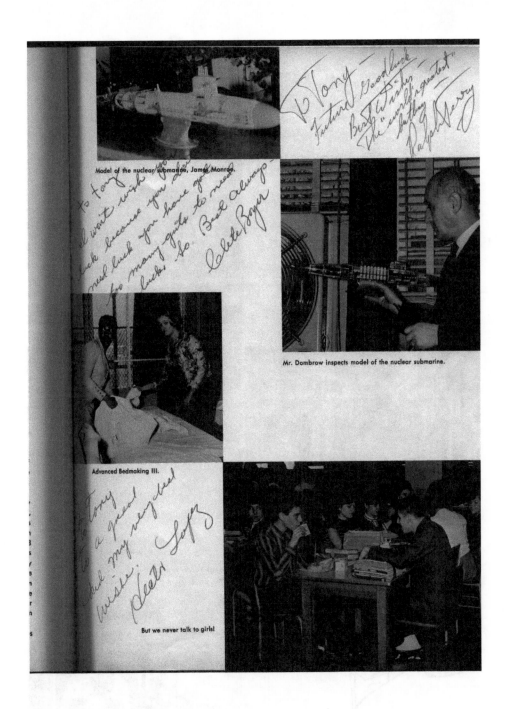

Model of the nuclear submarine, James Monroe.

Mr. Dombrow inspects model of the nuclear submarine.

Advanced Bedmaking III.

But we never talk to girls!

To Tony,
The hot dog.
Whitey Ford

To Tony
A Great guy
to work with
Greg

Biology Laboratory Group

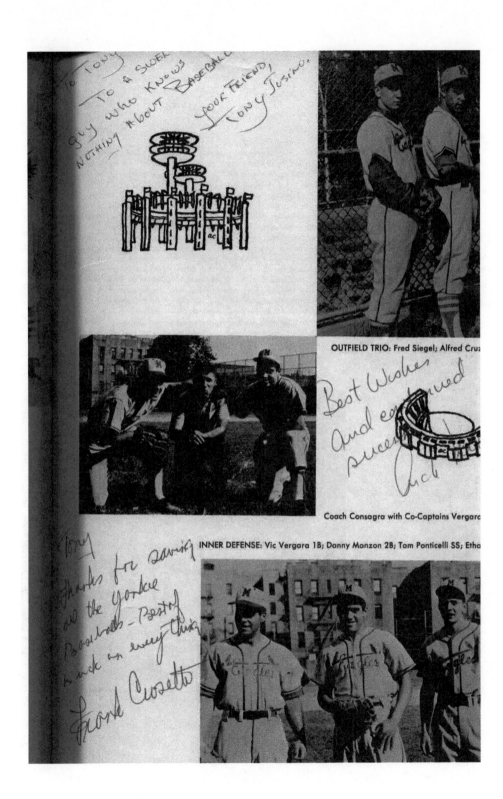

OUTFIELD TRIO: Fred Siegel; Alfred Cruz

Coach Consagra with Co-Captains Vergara

INNER DEFENSE: Vic Vergara 1B; Danny Monzon 2B; Tom Ponticelli SS; Etha

Swimming

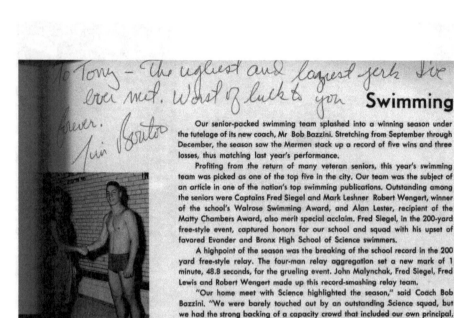

Our senior-packed swimming team splashed into a winning season under the tutelage of its new coach, Mr Bob Bazzini. Stretching from September through December, the season saw the Mermen stack up a record of five wins and three losses, thus matching last year's performance.

Profiting from the return of many veteran seniors, this year's swimming team was picked as one of the top five in the city. Our team was the subject of an article in one of the nation's top swimming publications. Outstanding among the seniors were Captains Fred Siegel and Mark Leshner Robert Wengert, winner of the school's Walrose Swimming Award, and Alan Lester, recipient of the Matty Chambers Award, also merit special acclaim. Fred Siegel, in the 200-yard free-style event, captured honors for our school and squad with his upset of favored Evander and Bronx High School of Science swimmers.

A highpoint of the season was the breaking of the school record in the 200 yard free-style relay. The four-man relay aggregation set a new mark of 1 minute, 48.8 seconds, for the grueling event. John Malynchak, Fred Siegel, Fred Lewis and Robert Wengert made up this record-smashing relay team.

"Our home meet with Science highlighted the season," said Coach Bob Bazzini. "We were barely touched out by an outstanding Science squad, but we had the strong backing of a capacity crowd that included our own principal, enthusiastic Mr Dombrow. His support, and the season-long backing of the students, was a great asset to the squad."

Captain Fred Siegel and Coach Bazzini.

SWIMMING TEAM: Left to Right—Mike Sandberg; Fred Siegel; Tom Spriser; Fred Lewis; Barrie Ross; Phil Balch; Alan Lester; Earl Weisert; John Malynchak; Robert Wengert.   69

...the responsibility...to respect the rights of others...

Best wishes
Tim Gleason

NATIONAL CONFERENCE OF
CHRISTIANS AND JEWS: *Left to
Right*—Marsha Slucker; German
Maisonet; Lourdes Garcia; Stuart
Shikiar; Mariana Lopez; Mr
Flaum; Eddie Kutner.

To Tony
The nicest guy I know
"All the luck in the world"
you Deserve everything you get.
From your
Good Friend
Phil Ling

Then go forty paces to the left ....

Mr Waldman and World History Class.

Social Studies Bulletin Board

Mr Irving Feirstein, chairman, provides Monroe's students with the opportunity to learn the art of ...ic. *Band, Orchestra, Choir, Chorus,* and *Dance Band* are musical offerings providing the student with ...ellent instruction, enhanced enjoyment and self-enrichment.

Courses in *Music History, Music Survey,* and *Basic Harmony* and *Theory* round out the available ...rings.

Our School Orchestra has received the singular honor of being invited to play at the World's Fair ...etime in the spring.

...e Band—Guy Lombardo wants us to fill in for him on weekends at The Fair

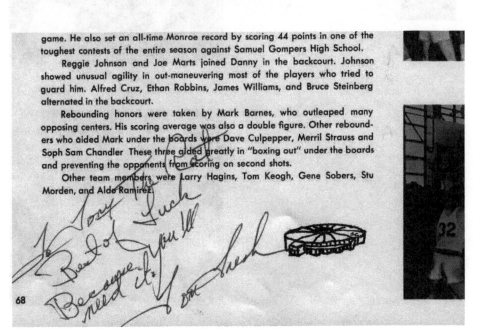

game. He also set an all-time Monroe record by scoring 44 points in one of the toughest contests of the entire season against Samuel Gompers High School.

Reggie Johnson and Joe Marts joined Danny in the backcourt. Johnson showed unusual agility in out-maneuvering most of the players who tried to guard him. Alfred Cruz, Ethan Robbins, James Williams, and Bruce Steinberg alternated in the backcourt.

Rebounding honors were taken by Mark Barnes, who outleaped many opposing centers. His scoring average was also a double figure. Other rebounders who aided Mark under the boards were Dave Culpepper, Merril Strauss and Soph Sam Chandler These three aided greatly in "boxing out" under the boards and preventing the opponents from scoring on second shots.

Other team members were Larry Hagins, Tom Keogh, Gene Sobers, Stu Morden, and Aldo Ramirez.

68

Senior Choir

Senior Band: No Strings.

s: Mr. Wiener   Orchestral Rehearsal Group.

116

Alma Mater

Beyond the city's noise and clamor,

Serene beneath the heaven's gold,

Clear in the radiant morning sunlight,

Our Alma Mater we behold.

To us, its loyal sons and daughters,

A glorious task it now shall be

To write in blazing crimson letters,

Monroe's fair history.

...Our youth are our greatest resource...

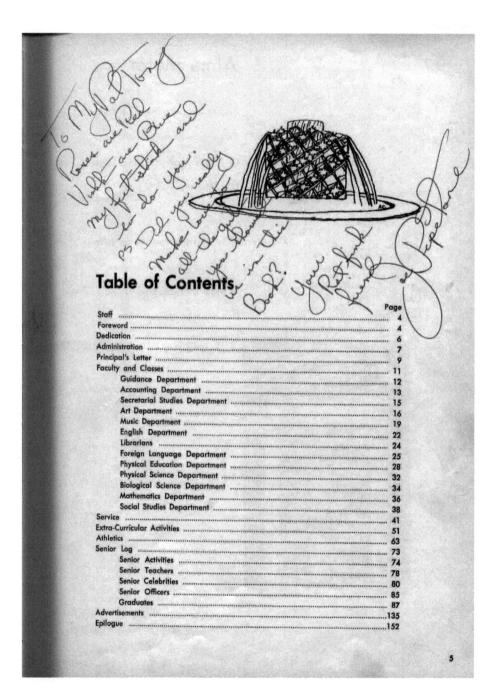

Table of Contents

5

118

To the old "curve baller"
Best of Luck Always

Your Pal
PeeWee Reese

To Tony I
wish you th
of everything
Chester Stamull

¿Habla Vd. español?

מזל טוב לכתה המסיימת

ITALIAN CLUB: Left to Right—
Mr Masella; Giovanna La-
Manica; Aida Cortez; Mar-
garet Stanullo; Rise Stam;
Virginia Giordano; Cathy Pi-
nelli; Laura Costa; Linda
Midiri.

MONROVIAN STAFF, JANUARY GRADUATES: First Row—Nancy Frankel; Sharon Cohen; Second Row—Connie Wantuck; Jessica Frank.

PHOTOGRAPHY CLUB: Left to Right—David Needle; David Ross; Barry Feldman; Mr Rosenkrantz; Richard Brodsky.

Basketball

Our Monroe Cagers came through the 1963-64 season with a 3-13 record. Led by the able coaching of Mr Sam Tolkoff, the Eagles gave many stronger teams a run for their money.

Captain Danny Monzon led the team in scoring, averaging 19 points per game. He also set an all-time Monroe record by scoring 44 points in one of the toughest contests of the entire season against Samuel Gompers High School.

Reggie Johnson and Joe Marts joined Danny in the backcourt. Johnson showed unusual agility in out-maneuvering most of the players who tried to guard him. Alfred Cruz, Ethan Robbins, James Williams, and Bruce Steinberg alternated in the backcourt.

Rebounding honors were taken by Mark Barnes, who outleaped many opposing centers. His scoring average was also a double figure. Other rebounders who aided Mark under the boards were Dave Culpepper, Merril Strauss and Soph Sam Chandler These three aided greatly in "boxing out" under the boards and preventing the opponents from scoring on second shots.

Other team members were Larry Hagins, Tom Keogh, Gene Sobers, Stu Morden, and Aldo Ramirez.

Cruz scores.

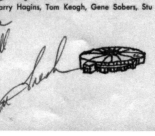

68

My Public

I may have felt that I was becoming somebody, but
to a number of adoring fans, to one very large television
audience and to millions of New York Daily News sports-
column aficionados, I really was somebody. It began in
my year as New York Yankee batboy in 1963, as fan-
mail started arriving at Yankee Stadium addressed to
New York Yankee Bat Boy and later to *Tony Florio,
Batboy.* Each postcard or letter confirmed that I was
not dreaming when I thought about what I was doing;
other people saw it too. Mail came in from across the
country, from boys and girls asking, begging and
pleading for my reply or for an autograph or, dare they
ask, for a photograph of me with one of the players; if
possible, with Mickey Mantle. All of the letters were
sweet and some were funny, always acknowledging
some fan's total amazement with my incredible good
fortune to be a bat boy. I was a thoughtful young man
and replied to as many of the letters as possible, and on
a special occasion, I would enclose an autographed
photograph of myself with one of the players. Some of
the letters came from young fans that had seen or had
even met me at one of the games; some came from fans
who knew me from school; each letter was an experience
in itself. A young fan from High Point, North Carolina
asking for autographs, photos and baseballs instructed
me to "Write back to me and tell me if you cannot send

me these things." Another fan from Philadelphia told me that he too planned to be a batboy one day and that he was only 5'2" and weighed 95 pounds; that he "expected to grow by April" and "how big should I be anyway?" A young girl from New Market, New Jersey whose sweatshirt I had personally autographed before a game at the Stadium submitted an enumerated list of questions for the Yankee batboy to answer:

1. How old are you and when do you have time to go to school?
2. When is your birthday and what is your home address?
3. How long have you been a bat boy and how long will you remain one?
4. Do you go on dates? Are you going steady with anyone?
5. When did you become a bat boy and for what purpose?

She went on to explain that my autograph was already coming off her sweatshirt and could she please have an autographed photo. A sixth grader from Hibbing, Minnesota asked for a number of items and closed by saying "and take it easy carrying the bats." A fourteen year old girl from North Merrick, New York told me that she had not yet found the boy she'd like to meet but "now I know that you are the boy." Ever popular with the young ladies one fan admitted to me that she was "an admirer in other ways, besides being a Yankee fan."

Some mail, having been intercepted by Big Pete or by one of the players, would reach me readdressed to me as *The Kissable Batboy, Fruitcup* and to The Personality Kid, Loveable, Creamsickle, after they got through reading it. One letter from a ten year old fan from Murphysboro, Illinois, also named Tony Florio, received quite a response from me. The letter also included a photograph of the boy and I was so impressed with the kid that I got in touch with his parents and arranged for them to attend the next game against the White Sox as my guests. When Little Tony came to the game at Comiskey Park, I brought him over to meet the Yankees and got him autographs from some of the players.

Certainly Little Tony Florio never forgot the experience, but I got just as much pleasure out of doing this for the kid, and after fifty years I can still remember the sparkle in his eyes and how much the experience meant to him.

A fourteen year old girl from Elizabeth, New Jersey stating several times in her letter that she was "clunky" told me how much she loved playing baseball as well as watching it, but assured me that she could "be very serious when she wants to be."   A favorite letter came from a little girl named Patty; a second grader from Newburgh, New York.   Little Patty wrote that she had seen me on television and wanted to know "How are you doing on your work?"   She also asked "May I have some of the Yankees' "*nams?*" as she spelled it and listed the names of fifteen Yankees, hoping for their autographs. Doing all of that writing probably exhausted the little girl because she closed her letter by simply saying "That's all. I am tired. Thank you."

The public also became familiar with me on a few other special occasions, one becoming a little bit more public than I would have liked. In August of 1963, after a three-game series against the Red Sox, I was sitting by myself on a flight to Chicago when someone came over and sat in the empty seat next to me. "You're Tony the Batboy aren't you?" asked the man. "Yes I am." I said. "Would you mind answering a few questions about being a batboy?" he asked. "Sure mister, I'd be happy to." The questions went on for quite a while and I really enjoyed the interest that this man had taken in my baseball experience, where I lived and where I went to school. He just kept peppering me with questions and I just loved answering them. Satisfied that he had gotten all the information that he needed, the man got up, thanked me and moved to another seat. As always I was polite and courteous to this older man but, as my street-smarts started to kick in, I also wondered why a strange guy would have so much interest in me and why he was asking all these questions. A minute later Elston Howard moved into the seat next to me. "Do you know who that was?" asked the great Yankee catcher. "He was a nice guy who asked me about being a batboy and some other stuff." I replied, wondering why Howard cared. "That nice guy was Mr. Dick Young" Howard explained. "One of the top sports writers in the country, who just happens to write a column for the New York Daily News and he may put something in his column about you." Not terribly impressed, I replied "No shit! I

124

wonder why he wanted to talk to me. I'm nobody." I didn't give it another thought until my mother called me a few days later. My mother sounded excited when I came to the phone. "What's the matter Ma?" I asked, expecting bad news. "Anthony" she went on "Do you know that you are in the newspaper today?" "What are talking about Ma?" "Anthony, you are in Dick Young's column today in the Daily News. In fact the entire column is written about you and about where you live and where you go to school and ..." I cut her off and said "Ma, can you read it to me?" My mother read the whole column to me and I could not believe that it really was all about me. Wow, I thought, this guy really believed that my experience with the Yankees was worth writing about. I thought about it on the plane ride but did not give it a lot of thought after that; until I went to school the following week. Back at school the shit had hit the fan. As soon as I got to school, Steve Ray approached me, waving Dick Young's column in his hand. "Anthony, do you realize how much trouble this column has caused?" he said. "Do you know that claims have been made by the other high schools that James Monroe has brought in a ringer from Manhattan, illegally; that they want us to forfeit all of the games that we won while you were on the Eagles; that we have broken all the rules!" I was speechless. Here it was that Steve Ray had gone out of his way to help me and to get me into Yankee Stadium and I had repaid him by bringing trouble to his doorstep; I really felt lousy about it. Fortunately for me, the matter was neutralized when Steve Ray proved to the other schools that, in fact, I never actually played

YOUNG IDEAS

By DICK YOUNG

YOUR WITNESS

(Do you swear that the answers you give are the truth, without circumvention or attempt to mislead? I do.)

Q: What is your name?
A: Anthony Florio.

Q: How old are you, Tony?
A: Sixteen.

Q: Occupation?
A: I'm batboy for the Yankees.

Q: How long have you had the job?
A: Since the start of this season. The other batboy quit because he was getting too old. He's 20.

Q: How do you get to be batboy for the Yankees?
A: Well, the head of the health educatoin department at James Monroe High, that's Steve Ray, he scouts for the Chicago White Sox, and he knows my father, who manages sandlot teams, and . . .

Q: What teams does your father manage?
A: Right now, the New York Redwings; they play all over the Bronx.

Q: You're from the Bronx?

From Little Italy to Yankee Stadium

A: Well, not really. I live in lower Manhattan, Mott Street; you know, "Little Italy."

Q: And you go to a Bronx High School? How come?
A: Well, I wanted to go to Monroe because they have a good baseball team, and I'm a pitcher. So, I used the address of a friend.

Q: I see. Do you pitch your father's team, too?
A: Well, I really can't pitch for anybody since I got this job, because I don't have time. But my dad has some good players. He had Kranepool and Duke Carmel playing for him.

Q: Let's get back to how you got the job. You were saying that this Steve Ray knew your father?
A: Yes, and he came to me in the gym office one day and asked me how I'd like to work in the visiting clubhouse at Yankee Stadium. And that's how I started, helping Mickey Rendine.

Q. How can you manage to go to school in the spring and still hold the batboy job?
A: They worked out a schedule for me at school where I finish by one o'clock. I go at 8, and I don't take a lunch period.

Q: You must be pretty hungry when you get to the park.
A: Yeah; I grab a sandwich, and put on my uniform, and go right to work as batboy. But during the summer, and for early night games, I get to the park about three hours before game time and help with the equipment.

Q: How much do you get paid?
A: A dollar-forty an hour. That's for game time, plus a half hour after.

".. AND A GREAT GUY, TOO."

Q: You don't get paid for those three hours before the game?
A: *No, but the guys in the clubhouse make up for that. They give me sandwiches and sodas and things, and some of the players tip you for getting them a snack like a hamburger, and at the end of the year you get a Series share.*
Q: You're sure of that?
A: *Well, with the Yankees you're pretty sure.*
Q: What do they vote the batboy?

Money is Good But So Is Road Trip

A: *Usually five hundred. But it's not the money. It's a great job and they take you on a trip once a year.*
Q: Are you enjoying this trip?
A: *You bet. It's the first time I've ever been away from home alone. Say, that Boston was something; everybody up there speaks like Mr. Kennedy.*
Q: Whom do they have you rooming with?
A: *Spud Murray, the batting practice pitcher. He's a great guy; always kidding around. All the ballplayers do. Pepitone and Linz treated me to dinner yesterday, and when I ordered a steak, they kidded me about taking the best thing on the menu.*
Q: Who is your favorite player?
A: *Mickey Mantle. He's the best in the world—and a great guy, too. They're all nice people—Maris, Berra, Crosetti.*
Q: Why do you mention them, specifically.
A: *They treat me like I'm one of them, and I think that's great because I'm the least important one around here, but they don't make me feel that way.*
Q: Doesn't anybody ever snap at you? Maybe when he's not going well, for example?
A: *Not yet. There's not one grouchy guy on the team.*

Must Learn Needs of Ballplayers

Q: In line with your work during a game, what little things did you have to learn about certain ballplayers' needs?
A: *Well, Yogi likes a lot of pine tar on his bat handle. Then, there's Kubek and Howard; they don't like to wear their helmets on the bases, so I have to be ready to grab them when they throw them away. And the pitchers, they like to use the bat of a guy who's going hot, so maybe I'll hand them a Linz model, or whoever it is.*
Q: Do you intend to be a professional ballplayer?
A: *Yes sir. I think it's one of the best jobs in the world, especially if you're good.*
Q: Are you good?
A: *I could be better; my control I mean. I'm working on it, and I'm being taught by some of the best—Bouton, Stafford, Crosetti. They all help me.*

one single game while I was on the team and that it was not necessary to forfeit any games. But the one thing that still baffles me to this day is why I was not thrown out of James Monroe High School after such an uproar. As proof of the expression that there is no such thing as bad press, I enjoyed even greater notoriety in Little Italy and at Yankee Stadium as word of Dick Young's column spread through the neighborhood and of my being able to continue at James Monroe; I was almost becoming somebody.

Reinforcing my public persona I was also lucky enough to become a regular guest on the *Red Barber Show*, which aired between games in double-headers. Double-header games were pretty common in those days; two games for the price of one. Today, fans have to pay for both games; the day game and then the night game. Being on the show also contributed to my fame and popularity in Little Italy, as more people in the neighborhood recognized the often-televised batboy and would come up to me on the street to say hello. The show was very popular and many of the players got a chance to appear on the program, but some of the players were never given the opportunity. One of the show's features was for guests to select a gift for appearing in a broadcast, based on the number of times they had been on the air. A one-time appearance may have earned a toaster for a guest, for example, or a camera for a three-time guest. One day after appearing on the show I studied the catalog looking at possible gifts to choose when one of the Yankees who had never

Red Barber interviewing Anthony for TV Show between a double header

been a guest on the show asked me why I was looking at the four-time page. "Because I've been on the show four times." I replied. "Why else would I be looking at that page?" Stunned that the batboy had been on the show as many times as Mickey Mantle, Yogi Berra and Whitey Ford, and that the player asking the question had never been on the rarely televised show – as few as ten double-headers per season – I received a cuff to the back of my head, sending my hat flying across the room. After having appeared on Red Barber's shows I was also interviewed by the great sports writer Jack O'Brian, who wrote some pretty nice stuff about me. Again, professional sports writers actually took an interest in me and what I had to say.

My largest public audience was not in any of the stadiums in which I performed as batboy and was in fact an audience that could see me but one that I could not see; at least not all of them. Having been contacted by the show's producers, I was invited to appear on the nationally syndicated, nationally televised program *To Tell the Truth,* hosted by the popular TV personality Bud Collier. The object of this game-show was for the secret guest to try to trick the celebrity panel into choosing one of the other contestants as the genuine article. After a series of questions the panel would have to vote for the contestant they believed to be the "real" person. As the secret guest, I was obliged to tell the truth. Not only was I going to appear on national television, I was also going to earn money by easily fooling the panelists, because on the show that day the

Jack O'Brian

ON THE AIR

Poor Cara

CONSIDERABLE MYSTERY has surrounded CBS-TV's decision to turn Keefe Brasselle, a somewhat commonplace actor, a bit puzzling as a singer, a rather earth-bound dancer, in fact a compendium of the second rate, into an Instant Irving Thalberg, with

Jack O'Brian

effusively announced plans for taking over TV, if not the world; therefore the appearance finally last night of his first production, "The Cara Williams Show," has been awaited with more than cursory interest in the trade . . . For Miss Williams has performed with carbonated efficiency and admirable comic spirit in other shows, a great many CBS hopes went riding on this new situation series . . . The backstage suspense now is over: it was terrible . . . Miss Williams isn't, but her comedy is, gags creaking and cracking instead of crackling, its humors steeped in early-talkie tricks and takes and cheap-quick comic cliches . . . Miss Williams plays a young office worker whose boss bars marriage between employes, so of course she is wed to another office slave, played by Frank Aletter . . . Its incredibilities lack the support of fresh new jokes and situations; you keep trying to place the antique situations and plot-tangles, to try and remember if Charlie Chase or some other hero of the low-budget 1930 movie-short era inflicted them first . . . It all rings false from its tinny laugh-track to the plodding impossibilities of its plots and strangled gags.

★

"THE PRESIDENCY: A Splendid Misery," a resourceful CBS research into the perplexities and bickering between U.S. Presidents and Congress and the Supreme Court and cabinets, offered in the very words of 35 men who have held the highest U.S. office, was a most interesting hour . . . Its staging was a trifle ostentatiously simple-modern, its play-actor Presidents dangling along a ganglia of flying wooden bridges and desks suspended high above the ground, where Frederic March most attractively and with earnest simplicity delivered the narration tying together the fascinating venom from snarling solons and harrumphing statesmen . . . The actors included Sidney Blackmer (fine), MacDonald Carey (good), James Daly (ditto), E. G. Marshall and Robert Ryan (both a bit inadequate in voice and as historical personalities, especially Ryan as Lincoln, which seemed like a small joke); and others . . . It was produced pretentiously but written shrewdly, even wisely, by Richard F. Siemanowski.

Pedro Ramos of the Yankees is the finest last-minute suspense-hero since Richard Talmadge and Rin Tin Tin . . . Yankee batboy Tony Florio, in the 'tween-game interview with Red Barber, gave a fine, interesting and informatively expert discourse on what bats which players use, their weights, dimensions and other unexpected variations on his batboy-job theme, laced with most intelligent observations . . . Fine TV interview.

panelists had to find the real New York Yankee batboy.
To prepare for the show I brought a ton of Yankee
equipment to the Manhattan studio – bats, hats,
uniforms, catcher's gear – all necessary to make me and
the two other kids look authentic. I also coached the
two other contestants on how to answer the questions, to
fool the panelists. The game began, but didn't last for
long, because I was a great batboy and a great spinner of
yarns but I was not a great actor.   Of the four panelists,
three out of four picked me as the real batboy and it was
Carol Channing, the great stage and screen actress, who
saw right through my thinly veiled attempt at being
evasive after all of the questioning. "He has to be the
real one." said Channing in her famous, raspy voice.
"He just looks like he gets excited easily." she exclaimed.
I received a lot of attention from being on the show, a
nice round of applause from the studio audience; I even
received more fan mail from people I had not heard from
in years, but I did not receive a lot of money from being
on the show. Having lasted only two rounds my total
financial reward for appearing on national television was
the minimum prize · $33.00 · and to make matters
worse I would now have to lug all of that gear back to
Yankee Stadium. I was on my honor, and Big Pete knew
every stitch of equipment that was in the Yankee
clubhouse anyway, but I wondered if it was worth being
on television and I sure wished I could have lightened
my load by giving some of that stuff to the two other
kids.

My Fan Mail

I enjoyed three great years at Yankee Stadium; 1962 as ball-boy for the visiting teams, then 1963 and 1964 as batboy for the New York Yankees. During my batboy years for the Yankees, having attracted attention from fans who attended games or from fans who watched games on television, I received a fair amount of mail from boys and girls from around the country. Some of the mail reached me without extra comments scribbled on the envelopes, but some fan mail was intercepted by a few Yankee players and those envelopes were editorialized and included funny or even harassing comments. I simply accepted this behavior as just another demonstration of how much the team really liked me.

The following pages provide a glimpse into a period in my life when I truly believed that I was the luckiest kid in the world, and by receiving such great fan mail, that other kids believed it too.

The notes and letters from kids close to my age at the time are most cherished, but the very warm and very sincere letter from Sister Paul Michel is by far, my very favorite piece of mail and I still read it every once in a while.

June 23, 1963

Dear batboy of the Yank's,

~ If you remember the Mayors Trofee game, you'll remember giving away Hector Lopez's bat to a boy. well I'm him. Yes, the boy you gave the bat to. I wish to thank you, I also wish to stay intouched with you. My name is Phillys. Please keep intouched; write soon.

Sincerely,
Phillys Sedinah

A thank you to Tony for Hector Lopez' bat

Oct. 3, 1964

Hi, Tony,

You'll probably think I'm a clunky girl for writing this, and won't read it but I don't care.

I wish I were as lucky as you to become batboy for the New York Yankees, but yeh! I know, I'm a girl! (a clunky one at that!)

I'm a nut about baseball and I don't care who knows it! The Yankees are my team, along with all the other New Yorkers who love them!

Once in a while my girl-friends get up a game. It's not really a game because we can't hit or field but you can't say we don't try! The boys have a 1000 laughs watching us, and if we get mad, we let them take over and we watch them! They are so much better than we are, but of course boys are always better than girls!

The reason I wrote to you, is because I'd like to have a personally autographed picture of you, if you'd please it to a clunky girl like me, when you get time)!

    You probably won't but you can't say I haven't tried! If you do send it please include your address, so I can send you a thank you-note! OK.

    Oh! If your girl gets mad at me for writing to you, please send me her address and I will clearly explain it to her! Thanks a million!!!

    Can you please send me you birthdate too, because I have a birthday book, and I'm collecting birthdays? Nutty but fun!

           Good luck forever!

           Mary Wnek
           ℅ Gloria Gilrain

P.S.) If you're wondering, I'm a 14 year old clunk who can be very serious when I wants to be!

Fan letter from a 14-year old fan

137

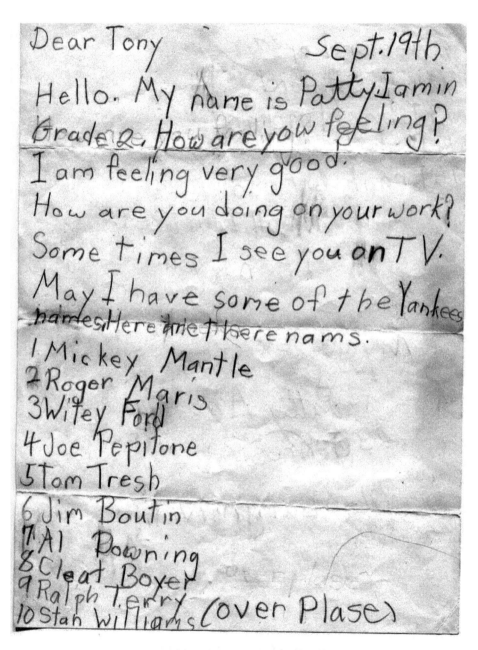

Dear Tony   Sept. 19th
Hello. My name is Patty. I am in
Grade 2. How are you feeling?
I am feeling very good.
How are you doing on your work?
Some times I see you on TV.
May I have some of the Yankees
names. Here are there nams.
1 Mickey Mantle
2 Roger Maris
3 Witey Ford
4 Joe Pepitone
5 Tom Tresh
6 Jim Boutin
7 Al Downing
8 Cleat Boyer
9 Ralph Terry
10 Stan Williams (over Plase)

Fan mail from a young fan

138

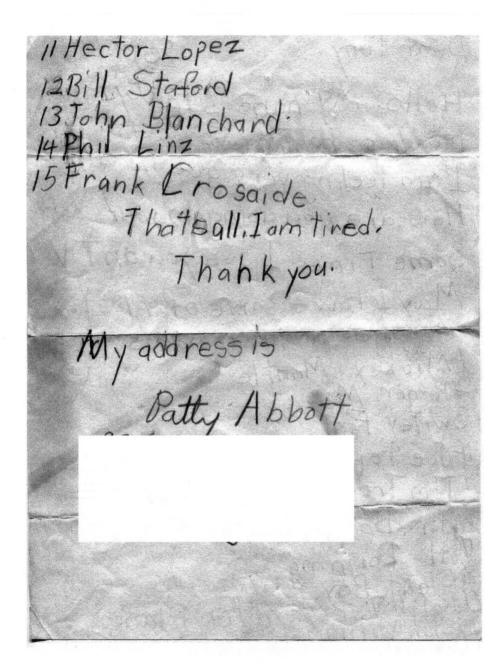

11 Hector Lopez
12 Bill Staford
13 John Blanchard.
14 Phil Linz
15 Frank Crosaide
      Thatsall, I am tired.
         Thank you.

   My address is

      Patty Abbott

Too tired to write more

Fan's letter to the "dark-haired Batboy"

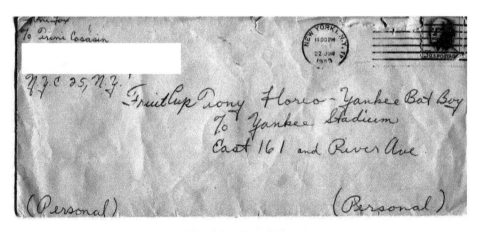

Edited envelope sent to Tony

Tony Florio

Dear Tony Florio,

I saw your picture in the paper and noticed your name is the same as mine. I am ten years old and am in the fith grade. I really would like to have your job, because the Yankees have always been my favorite team. I hope the Yankees win the World Series!

I live in a small town in Illinois and have never seen the Yankees play. Could you please send me a baseball signed by all the Yankees or if that is not possible, could you send me a picture of the team signed by all the players?

I am very glad we have the same name. Thankyou very much,

Your friend
Tony Florio

Fan mail from Tony Florio, fan, to Tony Florior, Batboy

September Newsletter   New York Yankee Fan Club
September 15, 1963   180 Vance Street
                             New Britain, Connecticut 06052

YANKEES WIN 28th PENNANT
    As you allready know, the Yankees have won the pennant. They won it on
Sept. 13, at Minnesota. The World Series will begin on Oct. 2nd in New York.
The Yankees opponent for the series, has not yet been decided.
    This was one of Yanks best seasons. Maybe the best because it was won
without their star players, who were out most of the time. Most of the credit goes to the Yank bench. Phil Linz, John Blanchard, Jack Reed, Harry Brig
and Yogi Berra all were valuable to the team. The Yanks had 2 pitchers who
won 20 or more games. Whitey Ford (23) and "Bulldog" Bouton (20). There
were many more stars, but lack of space enables us to print them all.
    We all wish the Yankees the best of luck in the series, and win or loose
they will always be tops with us.
YANK AVERAGES AS OF SEPT. 10.

Jake Gibbs 1.000	Joe Pepitone .275	Phil Linz .261
Pedro Gonzales .333	Tom Tresh .269	Tony Kubek .257
Mickey Mantle .322	Bob Rich'dson .266	Harry Bright .257
Yogi Berra .306	Hector Lopez .251	Clete Boyer .251
Elston Howard .286	Roger Maris .265	Jack Reed .230
		John Blanchard .226

PEN PAL SECTION

Sherry Jenkins	Margaret Abraham	Sue Price	Kathy Saluk
Route 1, Box 25	159 Monroe St.	8687 Grayfield	58 Slater Rd.
Sardis, Ga.	New Britain, Conn.	Dearborn 6, Mich.	New Britain, Conn.

Glenda Groman
26 Fernwood Rd.
New Britain, Conn.

ATTENTION ALL MEMBERS! CONTEST
    Here are the first 10 questions. Write the answers on a piece of paper
and send it to us, no later than Oct. 13, 1963. The answers of these 10 will
be in next months newsletter, along with ten new questions.(True or False)
Many of the questions will be on the Yanks. You will be allowed to use any
reference you you wish. Suggestions are any Yankee Yearbook, and books on
baseball.
Directions and Rules. 1. Any member can enter except for officers of the
club. Try and answer as many questions as you can. You DO NOT have to answer
them all. Send to Danell Cicella. All entries will be marked as soon as received, and in case of tie winner will be decided by postmark.
(1). Who was the Yankee Clipper?
(2). What were the Yankees first called?
(3). What former player on the Yankees won 4 most valuable player awards?
(4). What Yankee was known as "the Iron Horse"?
(5). What 3 Yankees have won 3 most valuable player awards?
(6). Who hit the most homeruns in one season? (154 games)
(7). How many pennants have the Yankees won. (not counting this year)
(8). Name the 3 present catchers on the Yanks.
(9). In what year did Babe Ruth hit 60 homeruns?
(10). What Yankee coach has been with the Yankees 32 years?
GOOD LUCK TO YOU ALL.   NEXT PAGE

Letter to Tony from an ardent fan of baseball

Dear Tony,

Will how are you? I hope fine.
I'm sorry I haven't been writing but
that is because of school. I think
I've seen every Yankee game on T.V.
except one. Will you be the batboy
in Kansas City Mo.? We get to
to go there when the Yankees do.
We also get to stay at the Muhle-
bach when You and the Yankees
go. I cant wait. Please write me
as soon as you have time. Will
better be closing I can't think
of anything else to say.
Love
Libby

P.S. Write soon
P.S.S. Sorry about the messy paper.
P.P.S.S. I've have several dreams about
you!

August 18, 1963

Dear Mr. Florio,(hope I can call you Tony),
    I am a great Yankee fan, and I try to learn almost everything
about the Yanks and about baseball. I've see every game on T.V. and
have seen all of the pre and post game shows Jerry Coleman and Red
Barba have done. Thats how I learned about some the players and how
I found out about you .
    I have written to you not to tell you about how much I know
about the Yanks and about how much of a fan I am , but to ask you for
a picture of you. Also if I can have a few words of information about
yourself,from you.
    Today in the Sunday news there was an artical on you in the
column of "Young Ideas", by Dick Young. I thought it was very interresting
and it told me a little more about you and you very interesting job.
It also said that you are a pitcher. I wish you all the luck in the
world ,and hope to see you pitch for the Yankees sometime.
    I know a few things about you and know what you look like
from my few visits to the stadium. You know nothing about me ,except
that I like the game of baseball. To tell you about me; I am 13 years
old , my hight is 5ft.,5in. I have ash blonde hair and chestnut brown
eyes . My ambition is to become a model.
    I hope this letter didn't take up to much of you time,but I
do hope you will beable to answer my letter by sending me your
picture ,and if possible a letter from you of the information I did'nt
read about in the paper.
    If possible to send your picture and information please send
it to me at the following address:(Thank You.)
        Miss. Sondra Strofield
        2 Amity St.
Rosebank,10305,Staten Island New York,N.Y.

                                        Yours truly,
                                        Sondra Strofield

P.S.good luck with your pitching. See you at the stadium!

<u>Take Us Out To The Ballgame</u> (Revised Edition)

Take us out to the ballgame
Take us out to the crowd
By us some peanuts and box row seats
The Yanks are awfully hard to beat
For it's root, root, root for our heroes
If they don't win it's a shame
For with Ralph Houk leading the boys
It's impossible to loose a game.

Mickey Mantle's our favorite
Roger Maris comes next
Joe Pepitone's from our neighborhood
Cletis Boyer is better than good
Bobby Richardson's handsome
Tony Kubek is cute
Elston Howard's the greatest there is
And we've Tom Tresh to boot.

Now it's time for our pitching
Whitey Ford heads the list
Bouton and Downing are coming up fast
Ralph Terry is good to the last
Root, root, root for relievers
Without them we would be lost
For it's Hamilton, Stafford and dear Kunk that make
The relievers boss.

The bench is headed by Phil Linz
Harry Bright is a doll
Hector Lopez is great in the clutch
Johnny Blanchard we love very much
Yogi Berra's Italian
That makes him loads of fun
And it's Reed and the rest of these boys
That make the Yankees number one

Now it's time for our batboy
Florio is his name
A great Yankee pitcher he'll be real soon
All the hitters will look out of tune
All the help he's been getting
Will sure pay off in the end
For it's Tony who will help the Yanks
Win the series once again.

(To be sung to the tune of Take Me out to the Ballgame)

Barbara Hegeras,

Dear Tony;

I doubt very much if you remember me but I'd like some information. Sunday when I went to the game at Yankee Stadium you autographed my sweat shirt for me. I asked you how you got to be a bat boy and you said it was a long story. Now that it's the time for the World Series I doubt if you'll have the time to tell me either, but whenever you do please write me and answer a few of my questions plus the one I mentioned before.

    1st - I'd like to know how old you are and when you have time to go to school, especially now during the World Series & for the few games in September?

    2nd - I'd like to know when your Birthday is and your home address? (In case I need it.)

    3rd - I'd like to know how long you've been a bat boy & how long you'll remain one?

    4th - I'd like to know if you go out on dates or go steady with any-one? (Probaly)

    5th - Althou this may be stupid to you, I'd like to know why you became a bat boy & for what purpose?

146

I don't know if you'll receive this letter because I don't have any idea where Yankee Stadium is; all I know is that it is near 161 St, and I can't put that on the envelope.

Another reason why I'd like you to write me is so I'll have your autograph when you sign the letter, in case anything happens to my sweat shirt! Your name is already coming off. If you have a picture of Yourself I'd like you to send it to me. (I'll even pay for it.) Well I guess that's all for now.

"Lots of Luck in

The World Series"

yours Sincerely,

Barbara Neveras

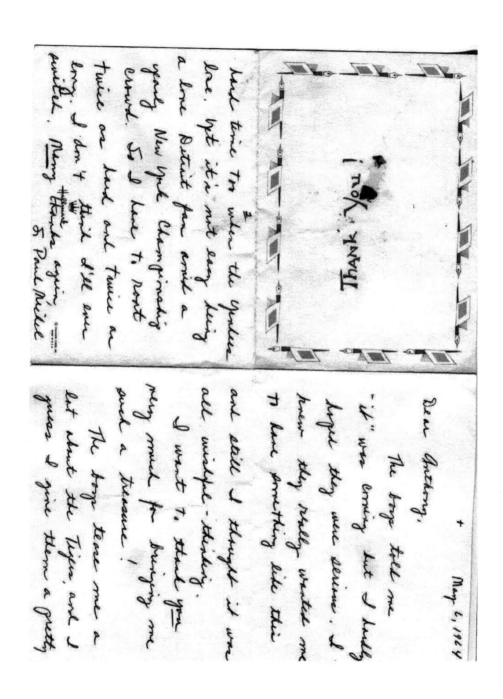

Thank you card from Sister Paul Michel for getting
her a Detroit Tigers autographed ball

The Mick and Me

Countless stories have been written about Mickey Mantle, from his early childhood days in Oklahoma to his final tragic days. How very lucky was I to have known him and to have worked with him so closely. My relationship with this courageous and gifted athlete is a more personal story, beginning in the 1963 baseball season and lasting through the end of the 1964 season. In those two short years I learned more about the human condition than in any other period in my life, as I observed one great man's struggle with debilitating physical challenges. With unparalleled admiration, the memory of my hero has sustained me for fifty years.

The two of us came from uniquely diverse backgrounds; a rural Midwestern farmland and an urban, densely populated metropolis. Oklahoma was famous for two things, as far as I was concerned; Mickey Mantle was born there in 1931 and some guy wrote a musical play about it, filled with songs about ranchers and cattlemen. As a young boy I learned as much about Mickey Mantle as I could, reading anything and everything to do with my hero – books, magazines, newspapers and baseball cards. One thing I learned was that as young boys, both of us were influenced by our father's love of the sport of baseball. *Mutt*, Mickey's father, loved the sport so much that he named his son after the great Philadelphia Athletics' catcher *Mickey Cochrane*, and that he spent every spare hour with young Mickey, teaching and training him to become a great ballplayer. My father loved the sport

Tony and his Hero, the Great Mickey Mantle

so much that he helped me to bend the rules
of high school admission so that I could attend a
school with a better baseball team. Father and son
relationships have peaks and valleys and each of us
could identify the exact moment when our fathers'
encouragement turned from influence into obsession.
Mutt chose to humiliate his son when Mickey couldn't
push himself any further. My father's dream of his son,
one day becoming a professional ballplayer, was of his
own manufacture, and his expectations for me were
much too high. When I had a bad day at a batting cage
one afternoon and could not connect well with the ball,
my father did not speak to me for a week. Fortunately I
redeemed myself at the same batting cage the following
week by hitting every pitch, convincing my father that I
had returned to normal.

   Before I would ever meet my hero, I read about him
and watched him on television as often as I could. The
networks got a lot for their money from Mickey
Mantle. By today's standards he was, in the 1960s, the
TV *super-star of the day*, equal in star-power to Derek
Jeter, Alex Rodriguez, Michael Jordan and Eli Manning
all rolled into one, but to me, more god-like than all of
them combined. In comparison to his predecessors
Ruth and Gehrig and even DiMaggio, Mantle earned a
good salary, but compared to the huge salaries and
endorsement contracts of today, he was grossly
underpaid and virtually ignored by corporate sponsors.
Comparing the huge salaries paid today, Mickey Mantle
earned as much in an entire season as the current stars

earn in one game.   He was the definitive American Hero of the day who married his high school sweetheart and loved his country and apple pie. I was such an avid fan and, other than my empathy with Mickey's physical challenges, I had no interest in my hero's struggle with alcohol or in his well-publicized mood swings. Like so many boys my own age, I saw only a powerful, blond haired bolt of lightning running around Yankee Stadium, smiling and tipping his hat to the crowd. I would have an amazing opportunity to meet my hero while he still had star-power and could still knock the cover off the ball, and in the three short seasons when I was part of the Yankee organization, I would become closer to him than most people would ever get to their own idol.

Mickey Mantle was supposed to become the next Joe DiMaggio – who Mickey would revere throughout his own career – but it would take some time for DiMaggio's impression on the New York fans and his reputation with the press to fade for Mickey to earn such respect from the public.   I respected Mickey almost as much as I admired him, and having a chance as Yankee batboy to get so close to him only served to increase those feelings. When the 1963 season began I was cautious about approaching my idol; not in a shy way but in a reverent and respectful way. What I would have never seen as a fan was how Mickey's legs would be taped and bandaged before each game, and how after each game he would need to soak in a hot tub to relieve the aches and pains. On May 22, 1963, the aches and pains must have gone away. On that day, facing Chick Stobbs and batting left -handed, Mickey smashed a towering line drive that travelled 370 feet before it hit the 115 foot façade over the bleachers. To this day the controversy continues as to whether the ball would have travelled more than 600 feet if it had not hit the façade. In 1953 at Griffith's Stadium, Mickey hit a home run that was measured at 565 feet. It was the first time in professional sports that the term *tape-measure home run* was recorded in history. It always seemed to be Mickey Mantle who was the man behind all of the legends and all of the great baseball stories of the day.

I was just a little kid in 1951, and I don't have any recollection of when and how Mickey Mantle hurt himself so terribly that year, and in all my time with him I never did or would ask him about it. It was in his very first World Series in 1951 when, as a rookie, Mickey was picked to play right field next to his idol, Joe DiMaggio, who covered center field so well. A fly ball soared to the outfield, as both DiMaggio and Mickey ran towards each other to try to make the catch. At the last minute DiMaggio waved Mantle away to make the catch. That momentary distraction caused Mickey to step into a drainage ditch in the outfield, catching the spike on his right foot and twisting his right leg horribly; tearing the cartilage in his right knee. Mickey had to be carried off the field on a stretcher. The crowd, it was said, roared their approval as he left the field, but

Mickey must have known that this particular injury would haunt him throughout his career.

By recognizing how much it hurt him to run for a fly ball or to try to beat out a throw to first, I developed a deeper respect for my hero. Even playing with bandaged legs, when batting left-handed, Mantle clocked at 3.1 seconds while running to first base! For me, as well as for a lot of fans, it was more exciting to see Mickey Mantle strike out than it was to see another batter hit a home run.

Mickey made me feel very comfortable in the clubhouse from the first day in 1963 when Big Pete introduced me to the team. Mickey Mantle was a friend to everyone in the clubhouse and on the team and contrary to popular opinion, was as close to Roger Maris, if not more so, than he was to any of the other Yankees. When I first met Roger, he seemed to come across as indifferent, almost distant or distracted, but after closely watching the *M&M Boys* I saw that Roger Maris was a very warm and very shy man, extremely close and respectful to his teammates but terribly misunderstood by the fans and by the press. It was only two seasons ago that Roger Maris had become so famous for hitting a record- breaking 61 home runs, but he never, at least in my presence, talked about it or acted special. The incredible opportunity of becoming close to my true hero Mickey Mantle was, at first, mind boggling, almost surreal, as I would tell him the most trivial things about school or girls, but Mickey would just joke with me about my experiences, making me feel very comfortable; helping to create a very warm and cordial atmosphere. Being on the field with Mickey Mantle during warm-ups and batting practice was most definitely surreal, bringing me into another world, entirely.

In the clubhouse I witnessed another side of my hero; that of eternal prankster. Little Eddie, a funny little guy who was always in the clubhouse, was the assistant to Bruce Henry, the *Travelling Secretary*; he was also a favorite target for Mickey's pranks. Little Eddie was a fastidious, nattily-dressed little man with a high-pitched voice, who always carried his personal belongings in a leather briefcase that was often the subject of the team's ridicule. To me, Little Eddie looked like a miniature version of Felix Unger from today's Odd Couple. One morning before the game Mickey confiscated the briefcase and I knew that trouble was on its way. First filling the case with water, Mickey then placed it into the deepest recess of the clubhouse freezer and headed out to the field. Poor Little Eddie was frantic and searched everywhere for his briefcase but came up empty-handed. The next day as everyone was milling about in the clubhouse Big Pete reached into the freezer and said "What the hell is this?" Placing the completely frozen briefcase on the big table Big Pete asked if anyone knew who the owner was.

Little Eddie's eyes bugged out of his head and he started screeching "You guys. You guys go too far." On another occasion Little Eddie was sent to the clubhouse to request that a ball be autographed by the whole team for one of the Yankee's largest sponsors, but it was Big Pete's turn to be the prankster. Everyone signed the ball and then Big Pete said "What can we put in the box instead of the ball to trick Little Eddie?" Mantle stepped right up and offered a rotting orange from the back of the snack table; Big Pete quickly inserted the orange into the box and handed it to Little Eddie who ran up to the press-box. Within fifteen minutes Little Eddie's screeching voice could be heard in the underground tunnel leading to the clubhouse. "You stinking guys! You rats!" screamed the little assistant. "Do you know what I looked like when that guy opened that damned box?" The clubhouse roared. "You guys made me look like a jerk in front of those people!" In one more incident Little Eddie was pretty shaken up by a prank in the clubhouse. The team had been on the road for a number of away games and some of the players were a bit weary from all of the travelling. As Mantle came into the clubhouse Little Eddie greeted him and welcomed him back home. "How are you Mick?" squeaked Little Eddie. Mickey Mantle spun around and practically knocked the little guy to the floor. "How am I? How am I!" growled The Mick. "I'll tell you how I am, you little runt. I found out that while I was out of town you were messing around with my wife!" And with this remark the powerful farm-boy from Oklahoma grabbed Little Eddie by his lapels and lifted him off the ground. "It's not true Mickey, I swear. It's not true. Somebody is trying to set me up. I don't even know where your wife lives. I swear!" Mickey lowered the poor guy, who almost collapsed when he put him down and said "Well I'd better never hear another word about it. And stay away from my wife anyway!" The whole clubhouse erupted into laughter as Little Eddie ran out of the room; Mickey was laughing the loudest.

One afternoon it was Johnny Blanchard's turn to be Mickey Mantle's target. Blanchard was the back-up catcher, behind Yogi Berra and Elston Howard, as well as a utility outfielder for the team, but he was very sensitive, almost paranoid about his chances of being traded by the Yankees. Johnny Blanchard was born in Minneapolis, Minnesota and debuted with the Yankees in 1955. His best year with the team was in 1961; batting 305 in 93 games and hitting a career high of 21 home runs. His very good year was however overshadowed by Roger Maris' record-breaking 61 home runs and Mickey Mantle's 54 home runs. On this day Blanchard was scheduled to start the game and was in high spirits as he took batting practice; to douse those spirits Mickey had something special in mind; something cruel even. Aware of Johnny Blanchard's paranoia, Mickey, who was sitting in the dugout with Yogi, signaled for me and together laid out their plan; I would run over to Blanchard and tell him that manager, Ralph Houk, wanted to see him in the manager's office. "C'mon Mick" I said. "He's gonna get awfully mad at me when he finds out it's just another one of your pranks." But Mickey wouldn't listen and told me to just do it. So I ran over to Blanchard. "Hey John, Ralph told me to tell you that he wants to speak with you in the manager's office." Fearing that this might have something to do with being traded, Blanchard turned pale, his face fell and his shoulders seemed to sag as he walked slowly towards the dugout, passing Mickey Mantle and Yogi Berra on the way. Blanchard's fears were not unfounded, because being called to the manager's office was often bad news for any player. As Blanchard walked past the dugout, Mickey tried not to look him in the eye, but as Blanchard drew closer to him, Mickey and Yogi began laughing uncontrollably. Realizing now that the whole thing was just another one of Mickey's cruel jokes, Johnny Blanchard smiled at him and just started shaking his head. "You guys just had to break my chops, didn't you?" Blanchard said with a laugh in his voice, admonishing both Mickey Mantle and Yogi Berra for having almost destroyed an otherwise pleasant afternoon. Like all of the Yankees who had been tricked by their fellow teammates, Johnny Blanchard just laughed off the entire prank.

A few days later it was my turn to be the victim of my hero's sense of humor. As the team was getting ready to go onto the field I could hear a few guys conspiring about something and before I knew what was happening several Yankees grabbed me, picked me up and turned me upside down. "Over here" I heard someone say, as they tied my feet and hung me from one of the casement windows in the clubhouse. Everyone was laughing and then my hero, Mickey Mantle, walked over to me and, as the blood was rushing to my head, with a few quick swipes of a *Magic Marker*, my idol added insult to injury by drawing a very nice mustache under my nose. Mickey then walked out of the clubhouse. I hung there for longer than I wanted to before Big Pete came back to the clubhouse to rescue me. I ran to the mirror to see Mickey's handiwork. "How the hell am I supposed to get this crap off my face?" Reaching for anything I could lay my hands on, I began scrubbing furiously – a brush used to clean spikes, a rag, even *Brillo*– until my skin was raw. As I went out to the field everyone was laughing at me because my face was as red as a beet, but I did not get angry. Such shenanigans were a rite of passage in the clubhouse and I could take it as well as I could dish it out. Also, I always truly believed that if the ballplayers did not mess around with me it would have meant that they really didn't like me. Well, whether I liked it or not, the Yankees really, really liked me that day.

Mickey continued to pull pranks even years after I left the team. On one occasion in the 1970s, Mickey did get his just reward. As I heard Mickey tell the story during a televised interview, Whitey Ford and Billy Martin had planned a deer hunting trip somewhere in Texas. They approached a large ranch, perfect for tracking Whitetail Deer, but weren't sure if they'd be allowed to hunt on the land. Billy Martin suggested that Mickey drive up to the farmhouse and ask the owner for permission to hunt. Mickey does so, goes into the man's house and speaks with him. Permission to hunt is granted by the rancher, with one request. An old mule needs to be put down and per the rancher, he just cannot shoot his own mule; would Mickey, being a big game hunter, please do the deed. He agreed and from the time he left the rancher's house and until he got back to the car, Mickey hatched a story to tell Billy Martin. "How'd it go?" asks Billy. "How'd it go? I'll tell you how it went." Lied Mickey. "That miserable old so and so is the nastiest SOB I have ever met. He cursed me out and said if we don't get off his property he'll start shooting at us!" Billy was shocked, as Mickey reached for his hunting rifle. "What the hell are you going to do?" Billy asked. "I'll fix that guy. Watch this." With that, Billy sees Mickey go right up to the mule and blow its brains out. As Mickey is standing over the dead mule he hears three more shots; at close range. Staring at Billy in total amazement he screams "What the hell did you do?" Billy says "Well, I saw how angry this guy made you and what you did, so I also shot three of his cows!" I can attest to the harmonica incident on the bus because I was there, and I was *not* with Mickey Mantle and Billy Martin when this incident was alleged to have taken place in the 1970s, but I can believe that it is a true story because of the way Mickey would pull pranks in the clubhouse and off the field.

While I was batboy for the Yankees I was very connected to Mickey Mantle, almost to the point where I truly believed that no one else could ever have felt about him the same way I did. But I did come to realize that he belonged to the public – to his public – and to history itself. One of the people I had a chance to meet when I was batboy who publicly shared his affection for The Mick was the great Yankee announcer Bob Sheppard. Mr. Sheppard was a fixture with the team; announcing for the team 20 years before I got there and continuing for at least another 20 years after I left. His voice, in my opinion, was and will always be the official voice of the New York Yankees. Bob Sheppard told the sportswriters of the day that when he announced Mickey Mantle's name as The Mick approached the batter's box, he felt a thrill that only Mickey Mantle could create; that Mickey Mantle was his favorite player to announce. On more than one occasion Mr. Sheppard would come into the clubhouse to say hello to the players and would always spend the most time with The Mick. One afternoon while I was tending to my batboy chores, Mr. Sheppard called my name in that great baritone voice and said "Hey Tony. Maybe one day I'll be announcing the name of Tony Florio, as you step into the batter's box!" I smiled from ear to ear and just said "Maybe one day you will Mr. Sheppard." The Mick smiled, pulled my hat over my eyes, and headed for the field.

The memories of the days spent with Mickey Mantle are still vivid in my mind, but none more so than the time when Mickey hit a ground ball to short and broke his foot while running to beat the throw to first. He just seemed to drop and the Stadium went silent as he fell. The broken bone in his foot and the injury kept him out of the lineup for weeks. After intense physical therapy and regular work outs – what seemed like a year to me – Mickey was placed back on the roster but was not in the starting lineup. Before the game Mickey went into the outfield with the rest of the team during batting practice to shag fly balls; I was right behind him as he went onto the field. As the balls were hit anywhere near me, Mickey would reach over, make the catch and just smile; even if I tried to run to make a catch, my hero was on top of it in a flash. This went on for a while and the fans were enjoying every minute of it, cheering with every catch that Mickey would make. As the cheering grew louder he turned to me and looking at me straight in my eyes he asked "Hey Tony. Why do they love me so much?" I stared right back and said "Well it can't be your looks, because then they would love me more than you!" Mickey let out a great laugh and after stealing a few more catches we both headed for the dugout. The game began and within a few innings the Yankees had fallen behind, struggling to get on base. Into the later innings the battle grew more intense and Yogi had to make some changes; offensively and defensively.   It was the bottom of the eighth and the first Yankee batter was coming to the plate, as I peered into the dugout.   Yogi had signaled for a pinch-hitter and the crowd was restlessly anticipating his choice.   I knew before the crowd and I immediately turned to the fans and slowly raised five fingers and then another two – Mickey Mantle was Yogi's choice and the crowd went wild.   Just watching Mickey Mantle take a few warmup swings in the on-deck circle was thrilling in itself, but not having seen him play for several weeks, the fans were on their feet when he walked to the plate. His classic batting stance seemed more impressive on that day, as he let the first pitch sail over home plate; probably to see what the pitcher had in his arsenal, I imagined, but one pitch was all that Mickey needed to assess this pitcher's stuff.   The next few seconds passed in a blur as Mickey connected with the ball so hard that it seemed to explode off his bat and rocket into the stands in left field. The pinch-hit home run was not only spectacular, it also tied the game and the fans went berserk. The second-best sight for any Mickey Mantle fan was to watch him trot around the bases after one of his incredible home runs; head down, arms in a jogger's position, powerful legs showing no sign of impairment. In his prime, Mickey Mantle was the personification of class; a great and noble athlete whose only purpose in life was to come through for the team. Today I laugh about the modern day, post home run antics – high-fives, chest-bumps, crazy handshakes – and try to imagine how foolish Mickey Mantle or Yogi Berra would have looked, had they carried on in such a manner.

I was absolutely beside myself as my hero came through for his team, for the crowd and especially for me, his biggest fan. When the Yankees took the field again, Mantle had been taken out of the game for defensive reasons and sat in the dugout to watch the rest of the game. When the inning was over I walked into the dugout and sat down on the bench next to my hero.
Mickey's blue eyes seemed even bluer as I leaned into him and said "That is why they love you so much!" He just smiled at me and the two of us sat back to watch the game.

If Mickey Mantle ever had a really bad day during the two seasons in which I was a Yankee batboy, I never noticed it, but I did see him lose his temper on two occasions. One afternoon, in a pivotal at-bat, having struck out in his last appearance at the plate, Mantle struck out again. Outwardly he did not appear any different than he normally did, but inside he was seething; he absolutely hated to let his team down. Mickey Mantle could swear with the best of them but he did not often swear or appear upset on the field. As he walked down the dugout steps to the clubhouse, however, his anger got the best of him and as Frank Crosetti and I sat nearby, Mickey threw a ferocious punch at the door leading to the clubhouse, cracking it and almost tearing it from its hinges. Crosetti looked at me and said "One day he might hurt someone or he might even hurt himself."

The other occasion took place in the clubhouse after the Yankees had lost the 1964 World Series in the seventh and final game. The embarrassment of the loss to the Dodgers in 1963 in four straight games had taken its toll on the team and Mickey really wanted to even things up against the Cardinals in 1964. Perhaps there was something inside that told him that this would be his last World Series as a New York Yankee or that 1964 would be the last year that the Yankees would win a Pennant while he was still on the team, but whatever was eating him up could be seen on his face. There was some chatter going on in the background when I noticed a reporter walking over to Mickey for a comment on the game. He did not lift his head or look at the reporter and quietly said "Leave me alone." Unfazed by Mickey's request the reporter continued to badger him, trying to get a quote from the great ballplayer, and then Mickey raised his head. I had never seen such a look on my hero's face, even when the pain in his legs was unbearable; his blue eyes turned to gray. In a deep, pained voice he stared at the reporter and said "Get away from me." The chatter stopped and the clubhouse now remained silent as the persistent reporter, recognizing that he should respect Mickey Mantle's request, slowly moved on to try to interview a different Yankee.

Mickey Mantle's threshold for physical pain was ten times higher than anyone I ever knew in my life, but his tolerance of emotional pain had its limits. Failing to carry his team to a World Series Championship was profoundly distressing to Mickey for two reasons. He truly believed that it was his personal obligation to help his team win every game and that by failing to do so at any time, he was solely responsible for the loss. And of paramount importance in every aspect of Mantle's life was his father's influence on how his son should always strive for perfection and never accept failure as an option. Mickey Mantle loved Mutt dearly but he could never tolerate his endless criticism. As I saw my hero in this light – uncharacteristically emotional, bitter and angry – I felt his pain because I knew how important it was for Mickey Mantle to win. This also evoked experiences with my own father and how terribly I felt whenever I might have screwed up. In such a weakened and vulnerable state Mickey appeared as a tragic figure and my respect for this great and powerful man grew deeper and my adoration grew stronger. This would be the last time that I would see my hero behind the scenes; the last time to speak with him so intimately in the dugout or to shag fly balls in the outfield; to see him pull a prank on a fellow Yankee. I would now comfort myself with the trappings of my unbelievable journey with Mickey Mantle and the New York Yankees – photographs, autographs, baseballs, bats and gloves – and I would forever be a Yankee fan and would never forget those two incredible years with The Mick.

The events following the 1964 season and that followed his retirement from baseball in 1968 were terribly upsetting to loyal Mickey Mantle fans; too disturbing to even think about for anyone who ever had a chance to see this great ballplayer in his prime. In keeping with his honest, larger than life character, Mickey Mantle was his own best, most objective critic, admitting that, by drinking as much and as often as he had, he further abused his already suffering body, underachieved in attaining his goals and shortened his great career by many years. Like so many of his fans, I felt then, and continue to imagine today, what he might have accomplished if he had not abused himself so much and continued to play for even a few more years. In one of his final press conferences, racked with pain and disease, Mickey's bittersweet attempt at self-deprecating humor "If I had known that I was going to live this long I would have taken better care of myself." was a sad commentary on the ravages of habitual drinking. Shortly before his death one of Mickey Mantle's final requests was made to the great country-western singer,

Roy Clark; to sing Yesterday When I Was Young at Mickey's funeral. Roy Clark did honor Mantle's request in 1995. The last line of the song is "The time has come for me to pay for yesterday, when I was young." Mickey Mantle's own sad and poignant final assessment of his life's work.

Mickey Mantle was only 63 years old when he died, but I will always remember the powerful thirtysomething blond haired bolt of lightning that touched my life in so many ways. First, as so many fans had, idolizing him from afar, and then right next to him, in person, in the clubhouse, in the dugout and, most memorably, on the field at Yankee Stadium. Sometimes I believe that I was the luckiest kid in the whole world.

Recollections

My years at Yankee Stadium and my travelling with the team did afford me a number of memorable eyewitness occasions; some of which will forever be locked away in my memory and some which can be more openly discussed. In fact, beyond just a few accounts of my more adult activity, most of my recollections are G-rated.

Within the clubhouse itself it can be said that a locker room environment was very much in evidence; salty language, innuendo and basic insanity were the order of the day. Some players were all business and did not partake in the banter and some others could be counted on to provide laughs. My contribution to the general well-being of the clubhouse attendees was treating the Yankees to songs, sung as I took showers. I did have a pretty decent voice, but often, as I regaled the team with a song about this or that, I would be treated to a chorus of expletives, suggesting that I pipe down or shut up altogether. On one occasion, my voice having improved greatly due to all the practice, I belted out a rendition of Bobby Vinton's *There, I've said It Again* and Coach Jim Hegan said "Hey Tony. You sounded better than you ever have." To which another player suggested not to encourage the young batboy.

Another guy who attracted some attention in the clubhouse was Joe Pepitone. Joe was only a few years older and, prior to my joining the Yankees, was generally considered to be the original Hot Dog. Joe Pepitone was a good-looking guy, even with his big Neapolitan nose, and went to great lengths to look good for his public. Perhaps the most time-consuming phase of Joe's clubhouse routine was his hair drying and hairstyling ritual. I never actually timed the event, but it would not be uncommon for Joe to be drying his hair as I headed for the showers, and then finding Joe, still standing at the mirror with the hair dryer when I came out of the shower. I never bugged Joe about this but was always amazed by his performance.

Roger Maris was one of the nicest guys to me in my role as batboy; just a very warm and likeable man. Roger Maris was born in Hibbing, Minnesota in 1934 and seemed destined to end up in professional football rather than baseball. As a result of his talents on the gridiron, Maris was recruited to play football for the University of Oklahoma, but after attending one semester at the school, he left to sign on with the Cleveland Indians' farm team. He made his major league debut with Cleveland in 1957 and in his very first year, hit his first home run; a grand slam! Roger Maris was well on his way to becoming a home run legend, a few years later in 1961.

Tom Tresh was another really likeable guy in the Yankee lineup. Born in Detroit, Michigan in 1938, Tresh was just a few years older than me and was easy to get along with. He signed with New York in 1961 and, in 1962, was one of only a few Yankee-rookies to play in the starting lineup on opening day; earning the title of Rookie of the Year. It would not be until 1996 that Derek Jeter would have that honor again.

One observation that I made while with the team, and one that stays with me today, has to do with Yogi Berra. I really liked Yogi and gravitated toward him regularly. He was a good manager and had been a very good ballplayer. As a hitter, Yogi had the reputation of being the best hitter of bad pitches; connecting with pitches that were outside of the strike zone and once getting a base hit by hitting a pitch that had bounced before reaching the plate. What baffled me, however, had nothing to do with Yogi himself, but with Yogi's wife, Carmen. Yogi Berra was a great guy, a great ballplayer and a great coach, but he was not what anyone would consider a leading man. Mrs. Berra, however, was absolutely stunning and I just could not get my mind around how Yogi had landed such a beautiful woman. And what was even more baffling to me was that she married him before he became a major league ballplayer. He was just a regular guy, which says something about how really nice a man Yogi truly is. During home games Mrs. Berra would sit near the Yankee dugout in the Manager's Box and I would tend to position myself so that I could stare at her. The Berra's had three fine boys, Larry, Dale and Tim, and Yogi would often bring them to games and into the clubhouse. Larry was only a few years younger than me and he would hang around with me and his brothers during some of the games. Dale Berra would also go on

Yogi Berra

Yogi Berra 2012

to play major league baseball; coached for a while by his own famous father. Yogi showed no partiality to his son and treated him fairly; as he did with all of his players.

I really enjoyed my behind the scenes vantage point and could not be happier than to get to know famous athletes on such a personal level. It was also a learning experience for me in another way. Before I ever stepped foot into Yankee Stadium, the only people I really knew were of Italian descent, from New York City. I don't think I would have ever gotten to know people from as far away as California or Minnesota or Missouri or South Carolina, if I had not had this incredible experience. It's true, the common bond was baseball, so everyone seemed to speak the same language, but in accents and dialects that I might never have heard. Fans could know only so much about a player, based on what was written about them or on what the newspapers would show in photographs. Very few people know that Mickey Mantle could throw an awesome knuckleball. I learned this firsthand when Mickey and I would have a catch near the dugout. On one occasion, after Mickey had thrown a series of incredible knuckleballs, I, a pretty capable pitcher and curveball thrower, threw my version of a knuckleball back to Mickey. Never one to let something pass, Mickey told me to stick to curveballs. Another thing about Mickey that, maybe, a very observant fan might have noticed; whenever Mickey would take the field and run to the outfield, he would never step on the white lines on the field. To this day players indulge their superstitions; like wearing the same hat or underwear for days, if they wore something during a winning streak. Phil Rizzuto used to stick chewing gum on the button of his hat.

Most of the players enjoyed each other's company on the field and in the dugout but would keep to themselves after a game. Two of the nicest guys on the team, Bobby Richardson and Tony Kubek, would continue the camaraderie and would often engage each other in conversation. Tony Kubek was also a resilient ballplayer; recovering nicely after getting hit in the throat by a ground ball in the 1960 World Series. Tony was very likeable and became a Yankee broadcaster after he stopped playing professional baseball. I always appreciated knowing that my first impression of guys like Richardson and Kubek, of their being genuinely good guys, was further evidenced in their personal friendship.

Getting to see a bit of the personal side of some of the players was a cherished benefit of my experience with the Yankees. Hector Lopez, born in Panama in 1929, was a very clean-cut guy whose taste in casual dress ran to colorful Hawaiian-style shirts. Hector was the second Panamanian to make it into the majors and the first Panamanian to manage a triple-A ball team. He was a great utility player, a great hitter and played in the outfield with Mickey Mantle. In addition to being a really nice guy, Roger Maris was also a snappy casual dresser; Phil Linz drove the latest model Ford Thunderbird and would often take me for a spin in his new car, and we became good friends, on and off the field.

   To me, Phil Linz was a real cool guy who had an active social life and as far as I was concerned, was someone to admire. In addition to driving nice cars, Phil also had a great apartment in Manhattan on 64th Street and First Avenue. I had been there on a number of occasions and he always said I could use his place if I ever needed to. He planned to move to a bigger place and told me he was looking at a spot that was not too far from the existing apartment. When he finally moved he told me where the new apartment was and I kept it in back of my mind. Around that time, I had my eye on a real beautiful girl from Manhattan; a girl who was about five years older than me. After a series of introductions, phone calls and casual meetings, I finally convinced her to go out with me and probably sealed the deal when I told her I had an apartment in town. "You have your own place in Manhattan?" she asked coyly. "Well," I lied, "I do have a roommate who's a professional ballplayer, but he's travelling around the country most of the time." So, we go out to a really nice dinner, have a few drinks and I said "Why don't we go back to my place for a nightcap?" The chemistry was good, the mood was right and she said "Okay, but just for a nightcap." My heart was pounding and my mind was reeling as we left the restaurant, and then it hit me. I forgot where Phil's new apartment was! "So where's your place?" she asked, as we walked down a few blocks. "Not far. Just a few more streets" I explained somewhat nervously. "What's wrong Tony?" she asked. "Well, it's a new place and we just got it, and I can't seem to remember which building it's in." I lied some more. "You don't know where you live?" I started stuttering and stammering and said "Let me just go into this drug store for a minute and make a call." Thank God I kept Phil's phone number with me as I ran to a phone booth. He picked up after a few rings and said "Where the hell are you? I was going to wait until you got here and then go meet some people." He laughed when I told him that I had forgotten the address and said to just hurry up. When we finally got to the apartment on the East Side, which was about three blocks away from his old apartment, the mood was totally destroyed. Phil let us in, introduced himself to my date, and said he was just leaving. She looked at him, then she looked at me, pretty much sized up the situation and said "Oh we'll be leaving right after you. Just need to powder my nose and then we're off. Right Tony?" So that night, my luckiest kid in New York luck, ran dry. I never heard from her again.

In the early 1960s a popular men's fashion was the Alpaca wool sweater, known for its loose fit, puffy sleeves and bright colors. A number of Yankees sported this particular fashion, as well as other popular fashions of the day, because famous ballplayers were always offered discounts on just about everything in the hope that those players would refer customers to the business owners. A number of Yankees encouraged me to travel to West 13th Street in Manhattan and to mention their names to the proprietor. So I took the trip and purchased two really nice sweaters for the discounted price of $12.00 each. Today, if you can even find Alpaca sweaters, you'd have to spend a few hundred dollars for one. I wore mine for years and always felt connected to the Yankees when I wore them.

The more personal, off the field observations did impact my experiences with the Yankees but my dugout and on the field observations remain the most treasured. One afternoon in the dugout, while discussing the great contemporary ballplayers, I kidded Mickey Mantle about the great Willie Mays. "Hey Mick, I gotta ask you. Is Mays as good as they say? I mean, well, are you as good as he is?" To which Mickey replied "Are you kidding me Tony? He is good, but I am a much better ballplayer than Willie Mays!" And then Mantle's voice trailed off in laughter. That was Mickey Mantle. Just a great guy who never bragged and was the definitive team-player. Stories about chewing tobacco are numerous, but my fondest recollection of this foul but popular product involves the Yankee relief pitcher, Marshall Bridges. I knew firsthand about the terribly bitter taste of chewing tobacco and, like a number of players, would attempt to cut the bitterness by adding bubble gum to the mix. Marshall Bridges did not cut his chaw with anything, so when he accidently swallowed his tobacco during a game, he just passed out and had to be carried off the field. A few years later Jim Bouton introduced an all bubble gum look-alike product called Big League Chew.

I'm sure Marshall Bridges wished that product was available when he was playing.

My experiences and observations while with the Yankees were, for the most part, devoid of the ugly side of human nature, but for one unfortunate occurrence. The 1960s marked the beginning of America's intolerance of racial hatred, but for too many communities in America, intolerance had not yet arrived and hatred was still the norm. Long before Elston Howard had ever worn a New York Yankee uniform, another African-American ballplayer named Jackie Robinson had broken through the whites-only barrier in professional baseball to become one of the greatest ballplayers of all time, but in certain ballparks around the country, grumbling might still have been heard whenever a black player took the field. On this occasion, more than grumbling was heard and it did not go unnoticed. When the all too familiar and ugly racial epithet was invoked as Howard took the field, a rush of Yankees, led by Mickey Mantle, headed toward the stands, but before Mickey could grab the guy, a cop intervened and escorted the culprit to the exit. That ugly scene evoked something in me that day that I had not thought about for a long time. When my father coached little league, there were kids on the team who came from all backgrounds; including a number of black kids. On more than one occasion my father would invite a few kids back to our apartment for a home-cooked meal. One afternoon, two of the black players joined us for Sunday dinner. We had a good old time, ate very well and just talked baseball. At one point my father said "Anthony, why don't you walk the guys down to the train station on Canal Street." Of course I agreed, and as we started walking from Broome to Canal, I noticed that people who knew me would say "You okay Anthony?" or "Everything good kid?" "Of course!" I said and kept walking. What I realized later was that in those days, we never saw black people walking through Little Italy, nor did I and my friends walk through black neighborhoods. Honestly, it wasn't something we talked about or gave a lot of thought to; it was just how things were in those days. I was never taught to hate anyone or anything and I guess that day, when that idiot yelled at Elston Howard, I felt just as terrible as Elston. Mickey Mantle was a farm boy from Oklahoma and I don't know if in his youth, was a poster-boy for racial harmony, but like every other New York Yankee, Elston Howard was Mickey's teammate and brother and that day, the guy in the stands was very lucky to have a cop come between him and The Mick.

One behind the scenes occurrence was rewarding to me in a more practical way. In no way did the salaries of the Yankee ballplayers in the 1960s come close to the salaries of today, but for the period the Yankees did alright. Whenever the team would go on the road they would collect a few dollars to give to me while I was away from home, and it was not uncommon for me to receive as much as $80.00 from the players. This was awfully good money for a young man to have in his pocket; to explore the local neighborhood or, if necessary, to entertain a lonely young lady who had to wait for her friends to arrive.

I saw a great deal while I was part of the Yankee organization and I had the time of my life, both on and off the field with the team. My memories are very fond and many of my observations can be discussed freely. For the few occasions where discretion would suggest that an observation remain private, I can stare at all of the team photographs and just smile.

In my opinion, I witnessed the greatest period in baseball history; the generation that followed Lou Gehrig and Babe Ruth and before muscle enhancing steroids came into fashion. The generation that gave us Mickey Mantle, Roger Maris, Willie Mays and Hank Aaron. Powerful, clean, likable, drug-free athletes who set a standard that so many players who followed could just not meet. I was there. I saw them play, right in front of my eyes. I was the luckiest kid in the world.

When the story about my life as a batboy was being written it seemed to stall for a period of time. In 2012, while sharing some of my experiences with my friend Warren, a very good customer, I was thrilled to learn that he actually enjoyed a relationship with Yogi Berra on a personal level. He then asked if I would like to see my old boss again. For the second time since I was first inspired to tell my story to the world, my enthusiasm reached an even higher level. "I would love to see Yogi Berra again!" I said. With that, my very kind customer reached for the phone, made the call and arranged the meeting. Within a few weeks I was told where and when the meeting would take place. On the day of the meeting I felt like I was fifteen years old again and that I was going to Yankee Stadium for the first time.

It had been fifty years since I had last seen him and Yogi Berra was now well into his eighties. He did not recognize me at first, but when I showed him several photographs of the two of us in Yankee uniforms, both fifty years younger, his eyes lit up and he honestly reacted as if he remembered me. I told Yogi about my family and what I'd been up to over the years, and I also told him that I was trying to finish a book about my days at Yankee Stadium. He was very kind to offer to read the story and to critique it; to the best of his ability.

To have had the great experiences that I enjoyed with this great and kind man and to have been given another chance to see him again and talk with him again is a gift that has come full circle.

The Post Season

If there is any truth in the theory that we are a product of our environment, that outside influences are equal to or possibly greater than one's own thoughts, beliefs and ideals, then I am living proof of such a theory. Like most young children my early childhood was shaped, if not controlled by the culture into which I was born, and by the influence of a southern European mentality – mother, father, family first. The Italian-American experience had the greatest impact on my early childhood as a first generation American, teaching me to be respectful, obedient and tolerant, as well as faithful to my Calabrian and Neapolitan heritage. Growing up in New York City's Little Italy, surrounded by great friends and by colorful personalities, aware of the neighborhood's underworld characters, privy to abundant, premium quality food and apprentice to the culinary arts, I am today a definitive product of that great environment. The experiences of early adolescence – school days, ball-playing and neighborhood friendships – have further influenced my life and have contributed positively to the development of my character and personality. While living at 384 Broome Street I developed early childhood friendships with James Bari, Anthony Vasallo and Delores and Dee Dee Lombardi, all four becoming part of my inner circle. Some of the more colorful characters in the neighborhood –true products of their environment – developed personas resulting from specific events or, often, based on physical characteristics, and bore defining street names; Joe Meatballs, Baby John, Cha Cha, Sallie Crabs, Louie Pigeon, Rocky Stones, Jake the Snake, Patsy Credit, Vinny Head and 5-Minute Charlie. My own street name, *Anthony Shoes,* had more than one derivation; I was one of the fastest kids in the neighborhood and would fly through the streets and also, my mother would often buy new shoes for me, attracting the attention of my neighborhood pals. Even my mother had a nickname in the neighborhood. When she and my father got married and moved into 384 Broome Street there were two other women living in the building who were also named Rose. Within days of moving in, my mother became known as *Rosie theBride;* a name that stayed with her throughout all of her years on Broome Street. Even today, as my mother enjoys being in her nineties, the name still sticks. The incredible experiences of my teenage years at Yankee Stadium, however, have had the greatest, most positive and longest lasting influence on my life.

To put my experience at Yankee Stadium into a modern day perspective, you must first select a category of celebrity or fame in which to look – humanitarian efforts, performing and visual arts, literary circles, medicine, academic achievement, science and technology, economic and commercial success or the world of sports – to try to comprehend the impact that the New York Yankees had on my life. For a young student of political science for example, intrigued and fascinated by historical, monumental world events, an opportunity to meet with Nelson Mandela for one day, to speak with him of his great struggle and accomplishments, would have a comparable effect on such a student for a lifetime. For a techie, computer-gaming whiz-kid, a chance to meet Bill Gates or Steve Jobs, to learn how they created all of those awesome software programs and developed so many incredible search engines – maybe even play an X-Box game with them – such an encounter would stay with that person forever. Surely a high school drama student would cherish an opportunity to receive acting tips from Robert De Niro or, perhaps, an opportunity to have breakfast with Martin Scorsese and learn firsthand how to try to become motivated for a particular role; even for just one day. As an important matter of neighborhood history, *Martin Scorsese* was born on *Elizabeth Street* and was a personal friend of my cousins Delores, Anna, Rose Lamantia, and their two brothers Jerry and Red, who also lived near Mr. Scorsese. And for the jock, for the high school athlete hoping one day to letter in the sport of his choice; to just have a catch with Derek Jeter, or to receive a pass from Eli Manning or to shoot some hoops with Michael Jordan, such an experience would be treasured in his memory and chronicled in the annals of his family's history.

My treasured, cherished experiences at Yankee Stadium, being with my larger than life heroes every day, speaking with them, joking with them, catching fly

balls with them, continued for three years and might
have even continued for one more year had events gone
in my favor.   There was a chance that I might have
continued as batboy in the 1965 season and that chance
hung on the possible success of Duke Carmel making the
team, as well as on very special consideration by the
Yankee Organization to permit me to stay with the team.
I had a number of reasons for wanting to
continue as batboy for the Yankees, but no reason was
as important as the simple fact that I absolutely loved
being with the team, travelling with them from city to
city and meeting so many beautiful young women along
the way. Another reason was that my father was about
to open his restaurant in Little Italy and the idea of
bringing famous New York Yankee ballplayers into the
restaurant would no doubt attract lots of other patrons.
In February of 1965 I went up to the Management Office
at Yankee Stadium to plead my case; and why not – I
had the time of my life with the Yankees and I did not
want it to end. The fact that I was now 18 years old and
was probably closer to the age of a rookie than I was to a
batboy did enter my mind but did not deter me from my
mission. During the interview I outlined my reasons for
wanting to stay with Yankees; I had greatly enjoyed my
role as batboy and was immensely grateful for the
experiences and lessons afforded me in this capacity, my
family had just opened a restaurant and as Yankee
batboy, I would be in a great position to promote the
business, and, with Duke Carmel about to join the team,
I, having been Carmel's batboy as a boy, would now be
the perfect batboy for new Yankee.

As a teenager Duke Carmel had played for my father on the DeMaro-Falcones and was an excellent ballplayer; at nine years old, I was his batboy at the time. Carmel had played for the St. Louis Cardinals and the New York Mets and was, in 1965, invited by the Yankees to come to spring training and I believed that Carmel was a shoe-in to make the team. At the camp, my last and best hope for staying with the Yankees was shattered because Carmel did not have a successful spring training experience and did not get signed onto the Yankee roster.

My experiences during the three years at Yankee Stadium, working with all of the New York Yankee greats of the day, witnessing three major League Pennants and attending three World Series events, were beyond any of my greatest expectations. I observed and learned so much during the years at the Stadium – Mickey Mantle overcoming a severe physical challenge and playing so incredibly well in spite of it, Jimmy Piersall grappling with the demons created by a bipolar disorder yet still performing like an all-star, Bobby Richardson remaining faithful to a higher, more powerful belief, suggesting that baseball was just a game – and I was genuinely grateful for and completely satisfied with my good and great fortune of having had such an incredible time in those years. I never saw, not even once, any of the illegal substances that have troubled so many of today's professional athletes and I never saw or even heard about drugs or steroids in the clubhouse, but unfortunately I did see the terrible effect that alcohol had on my hero's life. I did not want to let go of those great years, but at eighteen, my attention was turning more towards the young ladies, so my time would soon be totally occupied.

When I think about it today, I would have paid for the opportunity to have been part of such a famous professional baseball team, and to think that, in addition to the experiences, I was paid for my efforts is hard for me to believe. As ball-boy in 1962 and as batboy in 1963 and 1964, I received a base-pay of $1.25 per hour for as many hours as the game lasted, plus an extra hour per game based on a half-hour before and after each game. Whenever I travelled with the team I would receive $8.00 per day for meals, and for having attended two World Series events, I also received a bonus of $500 for each event; quite a bit of money in those days. As ball-boy in 1962 I also received tips from many of the visiting players, often as much as $20 per team. Of all of the teams for whom I was a ball boy, the Minnesota Twins were, by far, the most generous team to ever attend Yankee Stadium.

Florio's Restaurant did enjoy some success in its early years and in 1965 did attract at least two former New York Yankees. In my first year at the Stadium in 1962 as ball-boy I caught the attention of the great Yankee announcer *Phil Rizzuto*. Having stopped a line-drive foul ball by backhanding it, my catch invited a classic Rizzuto comment. "Holy cow!" exclaimed *The Scooter*. "Did you see the catch that kid just made on that foul ball?" Phil took a liking to me and continued to comment on my talents throughout the 1962 season.

He would also come down to the field during batting practice and on more than one occasion took time to show me how to bunt; left handed and right handed. I actually became a pretty good bunter, having been taught by such a great ballplayer. I stayed in touch with him until shortly before his death in 2007, having conversations about the Yankees and about life in general. One afternoon in my post-batboy position, I made my way up to the press-box to say hello to Phil. This also gave me the chance to bring my son Matthew with me to introduce him to a great Yankee ballplayer. Jumping on the opportunity, I told my old pal about my family's new restaurant on Grand Street in Little Italy, to which he agreed to come to the establishment in the not too distant future. On more than one occasion, when he would visit Little Italy, Phil would come to Florio's Restaurant and greatly enjoy the excellent, well prepared food, after which he would go across the street to Ferrara's for great pastries. Whenever he did show up he was always very generous to me. My other pal, Phil Linz, was also an entrepreneur and in 1965, in partnership with a *New York Giants* football player, opened a great nightclub called *Mr. Laffs.* Continuing the relationship between them, Florio's restaurant became a regular supplier of miniature pizzas to Mr. Laffs, but after only six months Linz stopped ordering them from me because he could not make any money selling them; the staff at Mr. Laffs kept eating them because they were that good. Florio's attracted a number of celebrities whenever they wanted very good pizza and calzones. *Ed Sullivan* came in a few times;

the comic *Jackie Leonard* always came in and the great actor *George Peppard* could also be seen eating at a table. *Kate Smith* loved the calzones, as did the great singer *Jerry Vale* and the TV host, *Sonny Fox.* One afternoon a very good looking young woman pulled up to Florio's, double parked on the street and came into the restaurant to order some calzones. I took her order and thought she looked familiar, but went about the business of frying the calzones in the very good peanut oil for which Florio's was famous. I kept staring at her and masterfully stating the obvious said "You're *Barbara Streisand,* aren't you?" To which she replied "Shush, please. I don't want to attract any attention!" Once the crispy ricotta and mozzarella-filled house specialties were ready I was happy to say "Here you go Barbara! These are on me!" Thanking me, Barbara Streisand offered a tip, which I waved off and then sent her on her way. She was very pretty and had a very cute figure. Another very famous, extremely beautiful celebrity was one of my favorite visitors. One afternoon my father received a call from an agent for the magnificent Italian actress, *Sophia Loren,* asking permission to do a photo-shoot for a fashion magazine in the restaurant. Of course he agreed and within a day or so the stunning Italian movie star arrived with an entourage of aides and photographers. There had to be hundreds of neighborhood guys waiting outside of Florio's that day, all hoping for just one look at this incredibly beautiful woman. As the shoot was being staged I approached her and said "Ms. Loren, I only have one request." "Please, tell me what it is." said the very beautiful actress. "Before you leave here I just have to give you a kiss!" "Certamente!" replied the movie star. She kept her word and I got my wish. I also got a kiss in return, and I must say, to have been kissed by Sophia Loren was one of the greatest thrills of my life.

When Florio's first opened, my father believed that I would convince all of my Yankee friends to come to the restaurant and that, in turn, the Yankees would attract customers who wanted hang around with famous ballplayers. To give me a sense of prominence in the restaurant, my father promised me the position of Maitre D', which I accepted with great enthusiasm. "What a great job. I don't have to do anything but greet and seat the customers!" The enthusiasm faded quickly. Whether it was the lack of Yankee patronage or just the activity in the restaurant, I was demoted to waiter within three weeks and was also expected to cook when necessary, but I performed my duties well and developed a keen sense of the restaurant business. One afternoon my father had to attend to business outside the restaurant so he left me in charge until he returned. Shortly after he left, I received a call from a woman who wanted to place a large order; five large pies and five large calzones. "Sure Miss" I said, pleased with accepting such an order. "You can pick them up in about forty five minutes. May I please have your name?" "*Nancy Sinatra*." replied the woman. I hesitated for a moment but had to ask "The Nancy Sinatra?" "Yes young man. I'll be there in forty five minutes." "Holy shit!" I said after she hung up. "Mrs. Frank Sinatra – formerly – coming to Florio's!" I immediately went to work to personally make the pies and the calzones, committed to cooking the very best I had ever made. While I was in the middle of the preparation my father returned to the restaurant and noticed me working diligently on the large order. "Who's this for?" he asked. "You're not gonna believe this, but Nancy Sinatra called right after you left and placed the order." My father stared at me in a way that only a father can and said "Anthony, I don't think you should make all these pies until she gets here. What if it's not really her? Maybe someone is breaking your chops." "I'm telling you it is Nancy Sinatra and I'm not gonna have her come and have nothing ready!" My father shook his head and just said "You'll be sorry." The pies and calzones were almost done when I saw a huge limousine pull up in front of the restaurant, and out stepped Nancy Sinatra. I was beaming with pride and just stared at my father; my eyes conveying I told you so! She came in, paid for the pies and I carried them out to the car, thanking her for her patronage and for helping me to prove to my father that I knew I was speaking to the real McCoy.

A celebrity from a different world was also a regular at Florio's, often coming in for a light meal. Little Italy was, of course, home to people from all walks of life, including members of the underworld. On this day, the underworld celebrity was a very well known, very well respected person in Little Italy and throughout

New York City; always accompanied by two very large, very intimidating characters, right out of central casting. Toward the end of his meal the famous diner would signal to me –in neighborhood sign-language – that he wanted a little wine, and I would always comply, quickly. The gentleman had not been well and hadn't been in Florio's for weeks. One afternoon he returned with his associates in tow and, after I had seated them, one of the associates told me discreetly not to bring any wine that day; doctor's orders! The meal progressed and sure enough, the wine-signal was given. I read the signal as I always had and proceeded to serve a nice glass of Chianti to my patron. As I left the table the large associate followed me and, in a menacing posture said "Didn't I just tell you not to bring any wine to the table?" Familiar with and unaffected by such posturing, I replied "You tell him that he can't have any wine today, because I sure as hell aint gonna tell him!" The conversation ended and the large associate returned to his table, shaking his head and mumbling.

Having become such good friends while I was batboy for the Yankees, I continued that friendship with Phil Linz after my years at the Stadium. One evening in 1965 James Bari and I went up to Mr. Laffs to have a drink and, as luck would have it, that night Mickey Mantle and a half dozen other Yankees were holding court at a table near the bar. The team was not off to a great start in the 1965 season and I walked over to say hello to my idol and to the team. "What the hell is going on with you guys this year?" I asked. They recognized me immediately and, having spent some time in the bar for the better part of the evening, started kidding with and jostling me. "Because for $100,000 I'll come back and straighten things out!" That remark invited a barrage of expletives from the team as well as a volley of crumpled napkins, stirrers and a few well thrown peanuts. It felt great to be with even a few members of the team and especially great to see Mickey Mantle again; to be old enough, now, to have a drink with my idol. It was also very enlightening for me to see my hero in this casual setting, drinking so much and carrying on as if he were not in public; as if he were not the most famous Yankee in town. Mickey was drinking rather heavily that night but insisted that the drinks tasted like "cherry water." "My daddy made the real stuff" said the Mick, as he finished one drink after the other as if they were Cokes.

The experience with the Yankees contributed greatly to everything I ever did after I left the team. My experience at Florio's Restaurant was somewhat bittersweet as the challenges of a family business adversely affected the relationship between my father and me. Seeking employment outside of the restaurant business, I embarked on a career in banking and stock brokerage, securing positions at *Manufacturers Hanover Trust, W.E. Hutton* and *Eastman-Dillon.* Rising to the position of Supervisor at Eastman-Dillon, I managed a staff of twelve people for the firm and recall how business was conducted in the old fashioned way; on paper, with actual shares of stock attached to each transaction.   I also recall how my experience with the Yankees, though it had absolutely nothing to do with any of the positions for which I applied, was so instrumental in the success of my securing every job that I ever had. Returning to my familial roots, in the 1970s I opened my own luncheonette in SOHO on Walker Street, where for eleven years I provided good, affordable meals for thousands of regular customers. I sold the luncheonette in the early 1980s and in keeping with my culinary skills, offered corporate catering services to businesses for office parties and other events. A few years later I opened another small restaurant in Hoboken, New Jersey and did fairly well at that location for about five years and then went into the real estate business in Hoboken, selling condominiums and cooperative apartments.

In addition to having been blessed with an incredible childhood I am also blessed with two wonderful sons; Anthony Jr., from a previous marriage, and Matthew, from my marriage to my beautiful wife Jackie. In 2013 I was further blessed with the birth of my grandson *Edward Peter Florio.* In the 1980s I was able to put to use my talents as a sandlot ballplayer as well as my personal experience with the New York Yankees, by coaching Matthew's and Anthony Junior's little league T-Ball team, and then coaching most of the teams as they grew older.   For the most part my little league experience was enjoyable and pleasant, sharing Yankee stories with the kids, sharing some of the tips I had received from the pros and encouraging both the parents and the kids to enjoy the game; to enjoy the moment. Like myself, most of these kids would never make it to the pros or even to the minors for that matter, so I would tell them to just have fun and try not to get hurt, and though I never experienced then, any of the headline violence that has occurred in some of today's children's sporting events, I did encounter one father who almost got out of line. Anthony Jr. and most of his teammates were around seven years of age when I was coaching the T-Ball team, but some of the older kids who did not make the more advanced teams were permitted to play with the younger kids. One kid, probably ten or eleven, could not hit a pitched ball but did okay when a ball was teed up. He was a pretty big kid, strong for his age, and when he connected with the ball he could hit a decent line drive. During one at-bat the kid really tagged one, almost knocking over the infielder who tried to catch it, so I told the younger infielders, who were around seven years old, not to try for any line drives hit by the older kids and to just let them go into the outfield. This safety-first strategy did not sit well with one of the fathers as he shouted out that I was treating the team like babies. I called time-out and walked over to the stands, directing my attention toward the loudmouth parent. "Do you really want to see one of these kids get hurt? Maybe even get a bloody nose or mouth? Is that what you want?" I was upset with the father's remarks. "How would you like to play third base and let me hit a few line drives to you and see how well you do?" I suggested to the parent who began to shrink on the bench. "If not, then just sit back, enjoy the

game and be quiet!"   I never believed in pushing the
kids unnecessarily, especially at such young ages.
Years later, when I coached my son Matthew in both
baseball and basketball, I always knew when to employ
the proper amount of encouragement and when not to
apply any at all.   I never forgot my father's silent
treatment for my not having performed well in the
batting cage that day and I was certainly not going to
carry on such behavior with Anthony Jr., Matthew or
with any of the other kids on the team. I hope both of
my sons were and are extremely proud of their father's
great accomplishments as ball-boy and as batboy at
Yankee Stadium, and include my experiences in any
conversation about sports. In the early 1990's Jackie
had taken Matthew to do some shopping at the Mill
Creek Mall in New Jersey and as they were about to
enter the McDonald's in the food court for lunch, five
year old Matthew began tugging at his mother's sleeve
saying "There's daddy! There's daddy!" "Your father's
working Matthew." said Jackie. "Someone probably
just looked like daddy."   But Matthew was insistent and
succeeded in pulling his mother over to the Hallmark
Card Store, pointing to a plaque in the window.   Jackie
took a closer look and sure enough, a plaque depicting
the 1964 New York Yankees, with a skinny batboy
named Tony Florio was on sale in the store, and young
Matthew recognized his daddy in the photograph. Of
course Jackie went into the store and, for $28.99,
purchased the plaque to give to me that Christmas. The
boys were always talking about their father's escapades
as batboy and I would often show up at school to back up

their stories and prove to some of the kids that I really was the batboy for the New York Yankees.

    I am consistently reminded about how very lucky I was to have had such wonderful experiences during my time with the Yankees. During a recent visit in 2009 to the Newport Mall in Jersey City, Jackie and I stopped in at an AT&T store to inquire about a feature on Jackie's cellular phone. A young man in his early 20s was happy to be of service and while describing the feature, asked if I knew the score of the Yankee game. "Are you a Yankee fan?" I asked. "Absolutely!" exclaimed the young man. "Who's your favorite player?" I asked, expecting to hear the name of Derek Jeter or Alex Rodriguez. "*Mickey Mantle!*" replied the twenty-something year old. "Mickey Mantle? How the heck do you even know who he was?" Shocked but also thrilled that such a young kid would have appreciated my own idol, I pumped the kid some more. "I love Mickey Mantle and I know everything about him. I only wish that I could have met him or could have seen him play ball at Yankee Stadium." I looked at Jackie, wondering if the conversation had been contrived. Of course it had not been, and not as if I needed this kid's validation of my unbelievable, unforgettable experience of a lifetime; of my days with Mickey Mantle and the New York Yankees. What I realized, as I told the young Yankee fan about those incredible years – 1962, 1963 and 1964 – and as I watched the kid's eyes widen and his mouth drop, that the more I talked about those fantastic experiences, the more I relived them, the more I believed, finally, that, maybe, I really was the luckiest kid in New York.

Today, I am gainfully employed by *Direct Waste Services,* a large environmental services company in New Jersey and not a single day goes by when I do not think about or speak about my experiences with the New York Yankees. Since the early 1960s I believe that the greatest New York Yankee team ever to be assembled was definitely the 1998 team, which included Derek Jeter, Jorge Posada, Andy Pettitte and Mariano Rivera. Thinking about my wonderful experiences with the team in the 1960s and imagining myself as a batboy for the New York Yankees today, I would have the same affection for the team as I did back then. Perhaps Derek Jeter would substitute as a modern-day Mickey Mantle, at least in terms of team spirit or as a great ballplayer, just not in the same way that The Mick instilled himself in and affected the skinny kid from Little Italy.

About the Authors

Anthony Florio and John Siclare met in 2009 after having been introduced by Carmen Sarro, a dear and mutual friend. Anthony longed to share his story with the world and John had been considering a formal writing project for some time. Committing Anthony's story to writing became a story unto itself.

Not practiced in the field of technology and unable to share information electronically at the time, Anthony resorted to cassette-tape recordings, invited his son Anthony Jr. to transfer taped recordings onto CD format, and gave the CDs to John. So, John listened, paused, wrote, listened, paused, wrote, and so on. Handwritten notes were read, edited, entered into a Word format, and printed drafts were returned to Anthony for review and further editing.

When Anthony and John were relatively comfortable with the result of their efforts, the process of approaching the publishing world began. Published authors, unpublished authors, literary agents, small publishing houses, large publishing houses, relatives, friends and business colleagues were all kind and charitable in their responses, but more or less discouraged further attempts in trying to publish a story about an unknown batboy from Little Italy, written by an unknown writer from New Jersey.

Six years later, because of Anthony Florio's perseverance, and with the capable assistance of McNally Jackson Books, Anthony's story is now available for the world to enjoy.

To reach Anthony Florio to schedule a book-signing or an interview, readers are invited to contact Anthony at anthonyrflorio@gmail.com Readers interested in developing their own memoir or biography are invited to contact John Siclare at johnsiclare@gmail.com

Acknowledgements

There are a number of people who supported, influenced and assisted the authors in bringing Anthony's story to printed form, but the story would not have been written if a dear friend named Carmen Sarro had not introduced the authors in 2009. To begin the process of writing a story for publication, the well-known writer and publisher, Louis Aronica, was instrumental in charting a course for the authors that served to create structure and format. Published writers, Donna Goldberg and Joseph Traum prepared the authors for what they were about to encounter in the publishing world, always encouraging perseverance and commitment. Attorney Edward Jaffe encouraged the authors to prepare for success in the project and created a Literary Property Agreement that documented the process. Richard Cucci and Ed Belling were early supporters of the project, introducing the authors to a fine publishing house that considered the story.

Of paramount importance to the story, for better or worse, was the influence of Sabato "Sal" Florio who drove his son to experience the three incredible years at Yankee Stadium. And no son can soldier through life without the influence of a loving mother. Rose Florio was one of Anthony's most important influencers throughout his life.

As the story began to take shape, the authors shared word of the project and received inspiration and support from friends and family, including Anthony Florio, Jr., who was instrumental in the production side of the project. Jacqueline Florio provided constant support and Matthew Florio provided inspiration. Dorothy Siclare provided inspiration and Grace

Siclare provided editing support. Frank and Jacqueline Pizza-menti are dear friends and influencers. Anthony Buovolo was an early supporter and offered important details about baseball history.

Friends and family who inspired and encouraged the completion of the story include:

James Quigney Jr	John Gunnello	Warren Ross
Joe Scarpinito	John Anselmo	Anthony Falesto
Keith Burkhardt	James Bari	Ernie Damiani
Salvatore Gandolfo	Maria Caputo	Manuel Alers
Jeff Bryk	Chris Dyson	Edward Florio
Michael Gonnelli	Yvonne Florio	Tina Florio
Danny White	David Larghi	Danny Mejias
Steve Dent	Dave Phillips	John D'Agostino

Friends and family who just wanted their names in the book include:

Anthony Santoro Sr.	Don Mahoney	John Kenny
Frank Friel	Chris Curko	Nilo Llanes
Joe Czernikowski	Alex Mendez	Dino Ciccotti
Anthony Giaquinta	Bill Petolino	Juan Quinones

Friends and co-workers at Farese Direct Waste.

The authors are also most grateful to Margaret and Jacob Harring at McNally Jackson Books for their patience, professionalism and dedication to the project and for contributing so much to the production of Anthony's story.

Finally, the 1962, 1963 and 1964 New York Yankees and all of the players, for the opportunity of a lifetime.